Rudgyard Story

A collection of designs
for hand knitting by
JO SHARP

Acknowledgements

Pattern Writing *Jenny Green, Debra Kinsey,
Wendy Richards, Lucia Russo, Coby Yzerman*

Knitting *Sonia Charewicz, Jenny Green, Lily De Roost,
Dorothy Harwood, Trish Kennedy, Connie O'Brien,
Francesca Greaves, Norma Beard, Leanne Prouse,
Hazel Heggie, Janice Darrah, Whitney Weaver*

Garment Finishing *Sonia Charewicz*

Styling *Jo Sharp, Andrew Markovs, Bronia Richards*

Photography *Jo Sharp, Andrew Markovs*

Photography Assistants *Bronia Richards, Lisa Thompson,
Leanne Prouse, Rita Markovs, Jack Markovs, Frances Thom*

Models *Ella Macdonald, Kathryn Fleay, Connie Reddie,
Lawrence Baird, Shamara Kubacz, Beau Neunuebel,
Jasmine & Joelle Thom*

Hair *Dateline Hair Design*

Make Up *Chrisy Byrne*

Film Processing *Rainbow Pro Photo Lab*

Book Design Collaboration
Stumpfel Shaw & Bronia Richards

Computer Consultant *Scott Parsons*

Printing Prep *CDC Graphics*

Printing *Frank Daniels Pty Ltd*

Thanks For Rudgyard Farm Research
Beryl Miller, Ron Proctor

Published by Jo Sharp Pty Ltd
P.O. Box 357 Albany 6330
Western Australia
©1998, All rights reserved
2nd Edition

ISBN 0-9587033-1-0

Contents

Chapter 1
Sitting and Knitting

This story is about a place
near my home called
Rudgyard Beach.
At Rudgyard you can sit
and knit under a tree,
whilst the bush wrens dance
all around. Its a place to rest and
to restore creativity.
Still, there are always those
who come to Rudgyard
and say...
"what's happening,
what shall we do?"
They leave on a jaunt
up the coast each day,
looking for a place to be,
to shop, to lunch,
but once I get to Rudgyard,
I never want to leave,
until I must
because
Rudgyard is a state of mind,
not just a place.

Chapter 2
Finding the Mystical Beach

A retired sea captain named
Paul Harrison travelled
from England to Australia
in 1913 with his wife to seek
his fortune.

He was granted land on the
banks of the Wilson Inlet,
near Albany in Western
Australia, where he planned to
start a dairy farm. Captain
Harrison named the land
"Rudgyard Farm" after his wife,
Sarah Speakman Rudgyard.

The farm backed onto a beach
of unusual and intense beauty.
A uniquely spiritual and
mystical landscape, the beach
had long been a sacred
camping & fishing place for the
indigenous people of the area,
such as the ancient Mineng and
Noongar tribes.

To this day, discreetly
inscribed symbols notating
tribal visits can be found on
the rocks along the beach.

General Pattern Instructions

TENSION

At the start of each pattern, the required tension is given. Before you begin knitting the garment, it is most important that you knit a tension square. Using the stitch and needles specified in pattern, cast on 40 sts and knit approx 40 rows. Lay work flat and without stretching, measure 10cm both vertically and horizontally with a ruler. Mark with pins. Count the stitches and rows in between the pins, these should match the required tension. If not, you will need to change your needle size. Smaller needles will bring the stitches closer together, larger needles will spread the work out. Incorrect tension will result in a mis-shapen garment.

SIZING

Sizes ranging between XS, **S**, **M**, L, XL, XXL are given for adult garments, while children's sizes are given by age. The bodice circumference measurements given in each pattern are calculated after a 2cm seam allowance is deducted. Size Diagram measurements have no seam allowance deducted. Note that the bodice width of a drop shoulder garment adds length to the sleeve as it falls down the shoulder. To ascertain which size to knit, use as a guide, a favourite old sweater which fits the intended wearer well. Compare the measurements of this garment with the measurements given in the pattern and choose the pattern size which most closely matches the existing garment. Note that some patterns are designed to fit snugly, whilst others are loose fitting. Each pattern is accompanied by a photograph and in most cases, for adult patterns, the garment modelled is the medium size.

YARN QUANTITIES

Quantities of yarn are based on average requirements using specified tension and Jo Sharp 8ply DK Pure Wool Hand Knitting Yarn. Responsibility cannot be accepted for finished garment if substitute yarns are used.

GRAPHS

Each square on a graph represents one stitch. Unless otherwise stated, graphs are worked in Stocking Stitch. When working from a graph, read odd rows (RS) from right to left and even rows (WS) from left to right. Each colour used on the graph is shown by a symbol or number which is notated in the Key of the pattern being knitted.

Graphs may be enlarged by photocopier, for easier reading.

DISCLAIMER

Due to the usual photographic and printing processes, garments illustrated in this book may appear different in colour from the yarn shades specified in the pattern. Please view actual yarn shades for accurate colour representation.

PATTERN QUERIES

Write to:

Jo Sharp Pty Ltd

PO Box 357 Albany 6330

Western Australia

Abbreviations

alt	alternate		Pb1	purl into back of next st.
approx	approximately		psso	pass slipped stitch over
beg	beginning		rem	remain/ing/der
cm	centimetre		rep	repeat
Col	Colour		rev	reverse/ing
cont	continue		RS	right side
CN	Cable needle		Sl	slip
dec	decrease		st/s	stitch/es
dia	diameter		st st	stocking stitch
foll	follow/ing/s		tbl	through back of loop
inc	increase		tog	together
incl.	inclusive		WS	wrong side
K	knit		yb	yarn back
K1B	insert needle through centre of st below next st on needle and knit this in the usual way, slipping the st. above off the needle at the same time		yf	yarn forward
			yon	yarn over needle
Kb1	knit into back of next st.		yrn	yarn around needle
M1	make one - pick up loop between sts and K into back of it			
mm	millimetre			
P	purl			
patt	pattern			

Anjuli Jacket

Anjuli Jacket, Cropped Version

ANJULI JACKET

Knitting Rating: Beginner.
A stylish cropped or long jacket with set-in sleeves and deep folded cuffs.
The striped fabric is easily knitted using mostly Garter stitch with simple colour combinations.

MEASUREMENTS

Sizes	S	(M	L	XL)	
To fit bust	80	90	100	110	cm
Bodice circumference	100	110	120	130	cm
Cropped bodice length	45.5	46.5	47.5	48.5	cm
Long bodice length	71.5	72.5	73.5	74.5	cm
Sleeve length (folded)	43	43	43	43	cm

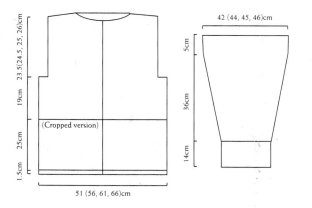

REQUIREMENTS
YARN
Jo Sharp 8 ply DK Pure Wool Hand Knitting Yarn.

No. Sizes	Colour	S	(M	L	XL)	
Cropped Jacket						
Col 1	Amethyst 503	6	6	7	7	x 50g balls
Col 2	Plum 505	3	3	3	4	x 50g balls
Col 3	Jade 316	2	2	2	3	x 50g balls
Col 4	Violet 319	6	6	6	7	x 50g balls
Col 5	Forest 318	1	2	2	2	x 50g balls
Long Jacket						
Col 1	Embers 804	7	7	7	8	x 50g balls
Col 2	Lichen 803	3	3	4	4	x 50g balls
Col 3	Amethyst 503	2	2	2	3	x 50g balls
Col 4	Owl 801	7	7	8	8	x 50g ball
Col 5	Wine 307	2	2	3	3	x 50g balls

NEED
1 pair
1 pair
1 Stitc

BUT
Cropp
Long

PATTERNS
TENSION
22.5 sts and 43 rows to 10cm, measured over patt, using 3.75mm needles.

COLOUR PATTERN REPEAT
Rows 1 to 4 Using Col 2, knit.
Row 5 K1 Col 2, * K1 Col 3, K1 Co1 2, rep from * to end.
Rows 6 to 8 Using Col 3, knit.
Rows 9 to 11 Using Col 4, knit.
Row 12 Using Col 4, purl.
Rows 13 to 18 Using Col 1, knit.
Row 19 K1 Col 1, * K1 Col 3, K1 Col 1, rep from * to end.
Rows 20 to 24 Using Col 4, knit.
Rows 25 to 28 Using Col 5, knit.
Row 29 K1 Col 5, * K1 Col 2, K1 Col 5, rep from * to end.
Rows 30 to 32 Using Col 2, knit.
Rep rows 9 to 24 incl, once.
Rep these 48 rows for patt.

LONG AND CROPPED JACKET
BACK
Using 3.25mm needles and Col 1 (*for version being knitted*), cast on 115(127,137,149)sts. Knit 5 rows garter st.
Change to 3.75mm needles.
Row 6 (RS) Working in Colour Patt (*above*), beg with row 1, work 86 rows for Cropped Jacket and 198 rows for Long Jacket.
Shape armholes Keeping patt correct, cast off 12 sts at beg of next 2 rows [91(103,113,125)sts]. Patt 98(102,106,110)rows.
Shape shoulders Keeping patt correct, cast off 11(12,14,15)sts at beg of next 4 rows, then 10(13,13,16)sts at beg of foll 2 rows. Leave rem 27(29,31,33)sts on st holder.

LEFT FRONT
Using 3.25mm needles and Col 1, cast on 63(69,75,81)sts.
Knit 5 rows garter st.
Change to 3.75mm needles.
Row 6 (RS) Working in Colour Patt (*above*), beg with row 1, work 86 rows for Cropped Jacket and 198 rows for Long Jacket.
Shape armhole Next row (RS) Cast off 12 sts, patt to end [51(57,63,69)sts]. Patt 72 rows.
Shape neck Next row (WS) cast off 10 sts, patt to end [41(47,53,59)sts].
Keeping patt correct, dec 1 st at neck edge in next and foll 8(9,11,12)alt rows [32(37,41,46) sts]. Patt 9(11,11,13)rows.
Shape shoulder Cast off 11(12,14,15)sts at beg of next row and foll alt row. Work 1 row. Cast off rem 10(13,13,16)sts.

Anjuli continued . . .

RIGHT FRONT
Using 3.25mm needles and Col 1, cast on 63(69,75,81)sts.
Knit 3 rows garter st.
Next 2 rows make buttonhole as follows;
Row 4 K3, cast off 3 sts, knit to end.
Row 5 Knit to last 3 sts, turn, cast on 3 sts, turn, K3.
Before continuing with this side, mark Left Front for position of
buttons as follows:
Button Placement (*5 buttons in Cropped Jacket & 7 buttons Long
Jacket*) space evenly with the top button placed on collar band.
Change to 3.75mm needles and knit Right Front to match Left
Front, keeping Colour Patt correct, reversing all shaping and
making button holes in positions marked.

SLEEVES
Using 3.25mm needles and Col 1, cast on 59(63,65,69)sts.
Knit 70 rows garter st.
Change to 3.75mm needles.
Row 71 (RS) Working in Colour Patt, work rows 19 to 48 incl,
then rep rows 1 to 48 incl for rem, AT THE SAME TIME shape
sides by inc 1 st at each end of 3rd row, then every foll 8th row
17 times [95(99,101,105)sts]. Patt 25 rows without shaping
[164 rows]. Mark each end of last row for end of sleeve seam.
Work another 24 rows patt. Cast off loosely.

MAKING UP
Press all pieces, very gently on WS using a warm iron over a
damp cloth, taking care not to flatten texture. Using
Backstitch, join shoulder seams. Place centre of sleeve to
shoulder seam and 24 rows above end of sleeve seam to sts cast
off at armholes on Back and Fronts and sew evenly in position.
Join side and sleeve seams, reversing seam for first 38 rows of
each cuff. Fold cuffs back.
Neckband With RS facing, using 3.25mm needles and Col 1,
pick up and K 28(32,34,38)sts evenly along right front neck
edge, knit across sts on back st holder, then pick up and K
28(32,34,38)sts evenly along left front neck edge
[83(93,99,109)sts].
Next row Knit to last 6 sts, cast off 3 sts, K3.
Next row K3, turn, cast on 3 sts, turn, knit to end.
[buttonhole]. Knit 3 rows garter st. Cast off loosely knitways.
Right Front Edging With RS facing, using 3.25mm needles
and Col 1, pick up and K 86 sts for Cropped version and
138sts for Long version evenly along front edge and across end
of neckband. Knit 1 row. Cast off knitways. Work same
edging on Left Front.
Sew buttons to Left Front to correspond with buttonholes on
Right Front, placing 4 sts in from front edging. Press seams.

Anjuli Jacket, Long Version (above left & right)

Bronzewing

BRONZEWING

Rating: Experienced with Intarsia knowledge.
A shawl collar cardigan with drop shoulder shaping, a bold Intarsia design and twisted rib bands.

MEASUREMENTS

Sizes	S	(M	L)	
To fit bust	80	90	100	cm
Bodice circumference	114	120	128	cm
Bodice length	49	51	52.5	cm
Sleeve length	44	44	44	cm

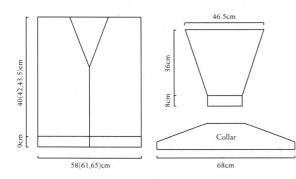

REQUIREMENTS

YARN

Jo Sharp 8 ply DK Pure Wool Hand Knitting Yarn

No.	Key	Colour	Yarn Quantity			
Sizes			S	(M	L)	
Col 1	❖	Antique 323	7	8	8	x 50g balls
Col 2	☐	Gold 320	6	6	6	x 50g balls
Col 3	✛	Lilac 324	1	1	1	x 50g balls
Col 4	▪	Earth 334	2	2	2	x 50g balls
Col 5	◥	Avocado 337	1	1	1	x 50g balls
Col 6	⊠	Olive 313	1	1	1	x 50g balls
Col 7	▣	Smoke 339	1	1	1	x 50g balls
Col 8	■	Slate 328	1	1	1	x 50g balls

NEEDLES

1 pair 3.75mm (UK 9) (USA 5)
1 pair 4.00mm (UK 8) (USA 6)

BUTTONS

4 x 2cm diameter.

PATTERN

TENSION

22.5 sts and 30 rows measured over 10cm of patterned
Stocking Stitch using 4.00mm needles.

CARDIGAN

BACK

Using 3.75mm needles and Col 1, cast on 130(138,146)sts.
Working in Twisted Rib as follows:
Row 1 *Kb2 P2 rep from * to last 2 sts. Kb2.
Row 2 P2 * Kb2 P2 rep from * to end.
Cont. in Twisted Rib for 9 cm ending with a WS row.
Change to 4.00mm needles and using st st, beg with a K row,
foll graph for Col changes. Work 122(126,130)rows.
Shape shoulders Cast off 8(9,10)sts at beg of next 10 rows.
Cast off rem 50(48,46)sts.

LEFT FRONT

Using 3.75mm needles and Col 1, cast on 64(68,72)sts.
Work 9cm in Twisted Rib ending with a WS row as follows:
Every row *Kb2 P2 rep from * to end.
Change to 4.00mm needles and using st st, beg with a K row,
foll graph for Col changes. Work 60(64,68)rows.
Shape front neck Keeping armhole edge straight, dec 1 st at
neck edge on next row and every foll 4th row, until there are
48(52,56)sts. Work 1 row.
Shape Shoulders Cast off 8(9,10)sts at beg of next and foll
alt rows [5 times]. Work 1 row. Cast off rem 8(7,6)sts.

RIGHT FRONT

Work as given for Left Front, rev all shaping and foll graph for
Right Front Col changes.

SLEEVES

Using 3.75mm needles and Col 1, cast on 54 sts. Work 8cm in
twisted rib as per Back, ending with a RS row.
Next row [inc] Rib 2, [M1, rib 5] 10 times, M1, rib 2 [65sts].
Change to 4.00mm needles and using st st, beg with a K row,
foll sleeve graph for Col changes. AT THE SAME TIME,
shape sides by inc 1 st at each end of 7th row, then one st each
end of the foll 6th row, 10 times, then foll 4th row, 9 times,
[105 sts] taking extra sts into patt as they occur. Work 5 rows
[108 rows]. Cast off loosely and evenly.

MAKING UP

Press all pieces, except ribbing, gently on WS using a warm
iron over a damp cloth. Using Backstitch, join shoulder seams.
Centre sleeves and join. Join side and sleeve seams using Edge
to Edge stitch on ribs.
Collar Using 4.00mm needles and Col 4, cast on 182 sts.
Row 1 * K2, P2, rep from * to last 2 sts, K2.
Row 2 * P2, K2, rep from * to last 2 sts, P2.
Change to Col 1 and cont in K2, P2 rib for 6 rows. Cast off 3
sts at beg of next 14 rows, then 4 sts at beg of next 22 rows,
keeping rib patt correct [52sts]. Cast off evenly in rib as set.
Using Edge to Edge stitch, attach cast off edge of collar piece
to neck hole.
Button band With RS facing, using 3.75mm needles and Col
1, pick up and K 70(74,76)sts evenly along Left Front from beg
of neck shaping to bottom edge. Work 6 rows in K2, P2 rib.
Change to Col 4 and work a further 2 rows in rib as set. Cast
off evenly in rib. Mark position on button band for 4 buttons,
the first to come 2cm up from lower edge, the last to come
2cm from top edge, and the remainder spaced evenly between.
Sew on buttons.
Button hole band Work as for button band, making button
holes to correspond with position of buttons. Sew the ends of
the bands to the collar. Press seams

Bush Wrens

Bush Wrens, Version 2
(see cap pattern page 27)

BUSH WRENS

Knitting Rating: Beginner.
A simple sweater or cardigan with drop shoulder shaping, folded cuffs
and easy to knit plain or striped Garter stitch fabric.

MEASUREMENTS

Children's Sweater & Cardigan

Sizes	3-4	(5-6	7-8	9-10	11-12	13-14)	
To fit chest	60	65	70	75	80	85	cm
Bodice circumference	85	90	95	100	104	109	cm
Bodice length	40	44	48	52	55	58	cm
Sleeve length (folded)	28	32	36	39	41	43	cm

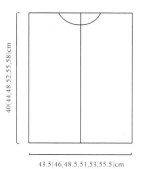
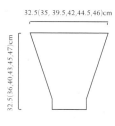

40(44,48,52,55,58)cm

43.5(46,48.5,51,53,55.5)cm

32.5(35, 39.5,42,44.5,46)cm

32.5(36,40,43,45,47)cm

REQUIREMENTS

YARN

Jo Sharp 8 ply DK Pure Wool Hand Knitting Yarn.

No.	Colour		3-4	(5-6	6-8	8-10	10-12	12-14) yo	
Sizes		Yarn quantity							
Sweater Version 1									
Col 1	Forest	318	7	8	8	8	8	9	x 50g balls
Col 2	Avocado	337	3	4	4	5	5	5	x 50g balls
Sweater Version 2									
Col 1	Violet	319	5	5	6	6	6	7	x 50g balls
Col 2	Wine	307	1	1	2	2	2	2	x 50g balls
Col 3	Cape	508	1	1	2	2	2	2	x 50g balls
Col 4	Terracotta	332	1	1	2	2	2	2	x 50g balls
Col 5	Brick	333	1	1	2	2	2	2	x 50g balls
Col 6	Miro	507	1	1	2	2	2	2	x 50g balls
Col 7	Rose	510	1	1	2	2	2	2	x 50g balls
Cardigan									
Col 1	Embers	804	11	12	12	12	13	13	x 50g balls

NEEDLES

1 pair 3.25mm (UK 10) (USA 3)
1 x 3.25 circular needle or a set of 4 double pointed needles for
sweater.

BUTTONS

4 or 5 x 2.5cm diameter

PATTERNS

TENSION

23 sts and 45 rows to 10cm measured over garter stitch using
3.25mm needles.

RAINBOW COLOUR SEQUENCE

Work 4 rows each of the following colours:
*Col 1/Violet 319,   Col 2/Wine 307,   Col 3/Cape 508,   Col
4/Terracotta 332,   Col 5/Brick 333,   Col 6/Miro 507,   Col
7/Rose 510**
Rep from * to ** throughout.

Bush Wrens, Cardigan

Bush Wrens, Version 1 (left)

SWEATER

BACK

(For version 1 and 2) Using 3.25 mm needles and Col 1 , cast on 100(106,112,118,122,128)sts. Work in garter st *(knit all rows)* throughout [for Version 1 in stripes of 4 rows Col 1, 4 rows Col 2 and for Version 2, follow Rainbow Colour Sequence on page 23] * work 180,(198,216,234,248,262)rows. Cast off.

FRONT

Work as given for Back to *.
Work 152(170,188,206,220,234)rows.
Shape front neck Work 41(44,47,50,52,55)sts, turn and leave rem sts on a st holder. Work each side of neck separately. Cast off 1 st at beg of next and every alt. row 9 times [32(35,38,41,43,46)sts]. Work 10 rows. Cast off. With RS facing, leave 18 sts on a st holder, rejoin yarn to rem sts and complete second side to match first side, rev all shaping.

SLEEVES

(for Versions 1 & 2) Using 3.25 mm needles and Col 1 throughout cast on 40(44,48,50,52,54)sts. Work 40 rows in Garter st, Row 41 inc 5sts evenly across row [45(49,53,55,57,59)sts]. Cont in garter st with 3.25mm needles, shaping sides by inc 1 st at each end of 7th row, then 1 st at each end of foll 6th rows 15(17,19,21,23,24)times [77,(85,93,99,105,109)sts].
Work 8(12,18,20,16,20)rows [146(162,180,194,202,212)rows]. *(adjust length here, if desired).* Cast off loosely and evenly.

MAKING UP

Press all pieces, gently on WS using a warm iron over a damp cloth. Using back stitch, join shoulder seams. Centre sleeves and join. With WS tog, using backstitch, join first 5cm of sleeve seam, then with RS tog cont joining sleeve and side seams*.
Neckband Using 3.25mm circular needle and Col 1, with RS facing, pick up and K20 sts down left side front neck, 18 sts from st holder across front neck, 20 sts up right side front neck and 38 sts across back neck [96 sts].
Row 1 & 2 Purl. Row 3 & 4 Knit. Row 5 Purl.
Cast off loosely purlwise. Press seams.

CARDIGAN

BACK

Using and 3.25 mm needles and Col 1, cast on 100(106,112,118,122,128)sts. Work 180(198,216,234,248,262) rows in garter st *(knit all rows)*. Cast off.

LEFT FRONT

Using 3.25mm needles and Col 1, cast on 53(56,59,62,64,67)sts. Work 153(171,189,207,221,235)rows in Garter stitch.
Shape front neck (WS) cast off 12sts, work to end of row. Dec 1 st at neck edge at beg of next and every alt row, 9 times 32(35,38,41,43,46)sts. Work 9 rows, cast off.

RIGHT FRONT

Work as for Left Front, rev all shaping working button hole as follows:
Row 9 Work 3 sts, cast off 3 sts, work to end.
Row 10 Work to last 3 sts, turn, cast on 3sts, turn, work to end.
Cont in patt working a further 3(3,3,4,4,4)buttonholes, the last to come 1.5cm from front neck shaping, the others spaced evenly between.

Bush Wrens, Version 2
(see cap pattern page 27)

SLEEVES

Work as for Sweater Sleeves.

MAKING UP

Work as for Sweater Making up to*. Sew on buttons to correspond with button holes. Press seams.

Bush Wrens, Cardigan (right)

Bush Wrens Cap, Children's

Bush Wrens Cap, Version 1

BUSH WRENS CAPS

Knitting Rating: Beginner.
A simple Garter stitch striped cap with Stocking stitch roll up brim.

MEASUREMENTS

Adult's & Children's Cap

Sizes	CHILDREN'S	(ADULT'S)	
Base circumference	52	57	cm
Crown to base depth	16	18	cm

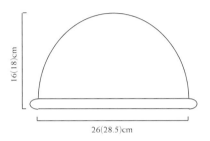

16(18)cm

26(28.5)cm

REQUIREMENTS

YARN

Jo Sharp DK 8ply PureWool Hand Knitting Yarn

No.	Colour	Yarn Quantity	

Adult's version 1

Col 1	Owl 801	2	x 50g balls
Col 2	Slate 328	1	x 50g ball

Adult's Version 2

Col 1	Embers 804	2	x 50g balls
Col 2	Terracotta 332	1	x 50g ball

Children's
Colour Sequence & Yarn Volumes

Col 1	Miro 507	1	x 50g ball
Col 2	Jade 316	1	x 50g ball
Col 3	Aegean 504	1	x 50g ball
Col 4	Wedgewood 340	1	x 50g ball
Col 5	Satin 311	1	x 50g ball
Col 6	Rose 510	1	x 50g ball
Col 7	Terracotta 332	1	x 50g ball

NEEDLES

1 pair 3.25mm (UK10) (USA 3)
1 pair 4.00mm (UK 8) (USA 6)

PATTERNS

TENSION

23sts & 45 rows to 10cm measured over Garter stitch using 3.25mm needles.

CAP

Using 3.25mm needle and Col 1, cast on 116(128)sts, work 6 rows st st. Change to 4.00mm needles and work a further 14 rows st st. Change to 3.25mm needles and alternating colours 1 and 2 every 4 rows throughout, beg with Col 2 [or for Child's Version, foll col sequence given throughout, beg with Col 2, working 4 rows each colour] K 32(40)rows.

Bush Wrens Cap, Version 2

Shape crown keeping patt correct;
Row 1 K1 * K3 tog, K16(18), rep from * to last st, K1 [104(116)sts]. Knit 3 rows.
Row 5 K1 *, K3 tog, K14(16), rep from *to last st, K1 [92(104)sts]. Knit 3 rows.
Cont dec this way until 20 sts rem. Knit 3 rows.
Next row K1(K2 tog) 9 times, K1(11sts).
Break off yarn and run end through rem sts. Draw up tightly and fasten off securely.

MAKING UP

Press cap gently on WS using a warm iron over a damp cloth, noting to omit brim. Using Backstitch, join seam, noting to rev seam for st st rows of brim. Allow brim to roll onto RS as illustrated. Press seam.

Crest

CREST

Knitting Rating: Average Skilled.
A comfortable waistcoat with Moss ribbed texture and "v"-neck shaping.

MEASUREMENTS

Sizes	WOMEN'S			MEN'S		
	S	(M	L	S	M	L)
	A	B	C	D	E	F
To fit bust/chest	80	90	100	95	105	115 cm
Bodice circumference	88	99	108	102	114	122 cm
Bodice length	46	47	48	58	59	60 cm

22.5(22.5,22.5,30.5,30.5,30.5)cm
2.5cm
21(22,23,25,26,27)cm
45(50.5,55,52,58,62)cm

REQUIREMENTS

YARN
Jo Sharp 8 ply DK Pure Wool Hand Knitting Yarn.

Colour			Yarn quantity			
Sizes	A	(B	C	D	E	F)
Women's						
Black 302	9	9	9			x 50g balls
Men's						
Owl 801				10	10	11	x 50g balls

NEEDLES
1 pair 3.25mm (UK 10) (USA 3)
1 pair 4.00mm (UK 8) (USA 6)

BUTTONS
Women's sizes - 4 x 1.5cm diameter.
Men's sizes - 5 x 1.5cm diameter.

PATTERNS

TENSION
35 sts and 33 rows to 10cm, measured over patt, using 4.00mm needles.

VESTS
BACK
Using 4.00mm needles, cast on 125(141,153,145,161,173)sts.
Row 1 K2, * P1, K1, rep from * to last st, K1.
Row 2 K1, * P1, K1, rep from * to end. Rep these 2 rows twice, then row 1 once.
Row 8 Inc in first st, rib 3, * inc in next st, rib 3, rep from * to last st, inc in last st [157(177,192,182,202,217)sts].
Beg patt - Row 1 P2, * K1, P1, K1, P2, rep from * to end.
Row 2 K2, * P3, K2, rep from * to end. These 2 rows form patt throughout.
Cont in patt until work measures 25(25,25,33,33,33)cm from beg, working last row on WS.
Shape armholes Keeping patt correct, cast off 11(14,16,11,14,16)sts at beg of next 2 rows [135(149,160,160,174,185)sts].
Dec 1 st at each end of every row 10(14,15,11,14,16) times [115(121,130,138,146,153)sts]. Work 48(48,51,61,62,64) rows patt.
Shape back neck Next row Patt 44(45,49,51,53,55)sts. Cast off next 27(31,32,36,40,43)sts, patt to end. Cont on last 44(45,49,51,53,55)sts.
Dec 1 st at neck edge in every row 8 times [36(37,41,43,45,47)sts].
Shape shoulder Cast off 11(12,13,14,14,15)sts at beg of next row and foll alt row, AT THE SAME TIME dec 1 st at neck edge in next 2 rows. Work 1 row.
Cast off rem 12(11,13,13,15,15)sts.
With WS facing, rejoin yarn to rem sts and complete second side to match first side, rev all shaping.

Crest continued ...

LEFT FRONT

Using 4.00mm needles, cast on 61(69,77,73,81,85)sts.
Work 7 rows rib as for Back.

Row 8 Inc in first st, rib 3, * inc in next st, rib 3, rep from *
to last st, inc in last st [77(87,97,92,102,107)sts]. Work in patt
as for Back until work measures same as Back to armholes,
working last row on WS.**

Shape armhole Keeping patt correct, cast off
11(14,16,11,14,16)sts at beg of next row
[66(73,81,81,88,91)sts]. Work 1 row.
Dec 1 st at armhole edge in every row 10(14,15,11,14,16)times
[56(59,66,70,74,75)sts]. Work 4(2,3,5,4,4)rows patt.

Shape front slope Dec 1 st at front edge (end) in next and
alt rows until 34(35,39,41,43,45)sts rem. Work
9(7,3,7,5,9)rows.

Shape shoulder Cast off 11(12,13,14,14,15)sts at beg of next
row and foll alt row. Work 1 row. Cast off rem
12(11,13,13,15,15)sts.

RIGHT FRONT

Work as for Left Front to **. Work 1 row.

Shape armhole Keeping patt correct, cast off
11(14,16,11,14,16)sts at beg of next row
[66(73,81,81,88,91)sts].
Dec 1 st at armhole edge in every row 10(14,15,11,14,16)times
[56(59,66,70,74,75)sts]. Work 4(2,3,5,4,4)rows patt.

Shape front slope Dec 1 st at front edge (beg) in next and
alt rows until 34(35,39,41,43,45)sts rem.
Work10(8,4,8,6,10)rows.

Shape shoulder Complete as for shoulder of Left Front.

MAKING UP

We do not recommend pressing this textured fabric. Using
Backstitch, join shoulder seams.

Front Band Using 3.25mm needles, cast on 9 sts.

Row 1 K2, (P1, K1) 3 times, K1.

Row 2 K1, (P1, K1) 4 times.

Rep these 2 rows 12 times [26 rows rib in all].

Buttonhole Next row Rib 4(4,4,3,3,3), cast off 2 sts, rib
3(3,3,4,4,4).
Next row Rib 3(3,3,4,4,4), turn, cast on 2 sts, turn, rib
4(4,4,3,3,3) [buttonhole]. Work 20 rows rib.
Rep last 22 rows 1(2,2,3,3,3)times, then buttonhole rows once
[3(4,4,5,5,5) buttonholes in all].
Cont in rib without further buttonholes until band is length
required to fit (slightly stretched) along both fronts and
around back neck. Cast off in rib.

Armhole Bands Work as for Front Band, omitting
buttonholes, until work is length required to fit (slightly
stretched) around armhole. Cast off in rib. Using Backstitch,
sew front band in position, placing buttonholes to right front
for women's sizes and left front for men's sizes. Sew armhole
bands in position, beg and ending at underarm. Join side and
armhole band seams. Sew on buttons to correspond with
buttonholes. Press seams.

Crest, Women's Vest (right)

Chapter 3
A Sense of Peace

On warm afternoons, people make their way onto the beach with food and friends to play and talk away the day, lulled by the peace, the lapping water and the bird calls. Their speech is languid and their topics inconsequential, while children play endless imaginative games along the shore.

Visitors to Rudgyard Beach become entranced with the feeling of the place. The unusually coarse texture of the beach sand is like small pebbles. The feel of this sand on skin, especially on warm days, is indescribably pleasurable.
The water is shallow, warm and amber in hue, like a nourishing bowl of miso soup with aromatic seaweed and mussels.

Smooth and shiny megalithic rocks at the waters edge appear as though some huge hand has come down from the sky to place and polish them. They seem to have been born of some ancient happening creating their mysterious sculptured forms.

A gentle wooded wilderness meets the beach in every direction, muffling all sound and providing shelter.
Many small birds and animals find their homes in this nurturing landscape.

At the days end the fires are lit, bats fly overhead to announce the dusk and stars begin to fill the spaces in the gnarled leafy canopy of Jarrah and Marri trees behind the beach. The story telling and singing begins and goes late into the night.

Harmony

Harmony

Harmony Child's Sweater, Version 2

Harmony Child's Sweater, Version 1

Harmony Men's Sweater (right)

HARMONY

Knitting Rating: Experience with Intarsia necessary.
A loose fitting drop shoulder sweater with minimal shaping, sized for all the family.

MEASUREMENTS

Adult Sweater

Unisex sizing

Unisex sizing gives a single S, M or L bodice width measurement to be shared by men and women. The medium measurement given for a woman's loose fitting garment is also the medium measurement given for the medium men's garment that will be worn slightly shorter and more snug fitting. Because men generally prefer garments to be comparatively shorter and to fit more snugly than women, the dual sizing given accommodates both sexes. Unisex sizing gives a separate sleeve for both men and women.

Sizes (Unisex)	S	(M	L)	
To fit women's bust	80	90	100	cm
To fit men's chest	95	105	115	cm
Bodice circumference Unisex	117	124	131	cm
Bodice length Unisex	70	70	70	cm
Sleeve length womens (mens)	42(49)	42(49)	42(49)	cm

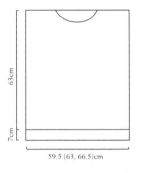

63cm
7cm
59.5 (63, 66.5)cm

46.5(50)cm
36(43)cm
6cm

Children's Sweaters

Sizes	3-4 yo	(5-6 yo	7-8yo)	
To fit chest	60	65	70	cm
Bodice width	83	90	97	cm
Bodice length	41	45	48	cm
Sleeve length	27	29	32.5	cm

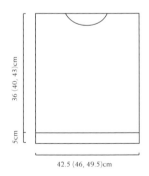

36 (40, 43)cm
5cm
42.5 (46, 49.5)cm

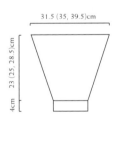

31.5 (35, 39.5)cm
23 (25, 28.5)cm
4cm

REQUIREMENTS

YARN

Jo Sharp DK (8 ply) Pure Wool Hand Knitting Yarn.

No.	Key	Colour	Yarn quantity			
Sizes			S	M	L	

Women's Sweater

No.	Key	Colour	S	M	L	
Col 1	☐	Natural 301	5	5	6	x 50g balls
Col 2	☐	Antique 323	3	3	4	x 50g balls
Col 3	☐	Satin 311	3	3	3	x 50g balls
	+	Lilac 324	1	1	1	x 50g balls
	⌂	Avocado 337	3	3	4	x 50g balls
	◊	Linen 335	1	1	2	x 50g balls
	■	Citrus 509	1	1	2	x 50g balls
	♣	Daisy 315	3	3	4	x 50g balls
	▪	Pearlshell 338	3	3	4	x 50g balls

Men's Sweater

No.	Key	Colour	S	M	L	
Col 1	☐	Owl 801	6	6	6	x 50g balls
Col 2	☐	Slate 328	4	4	4	x 50g balls
Col 3	☐	Eucalypt 502	3	3	3	x 50g balls
	+	Linen 335	1	1	1	x 50g balls
	⌂	Mulberry 325	4	4	4	x 50g balls
	◊	Ginger 322	2	2	2	x 50g balls
	■	Chestnut 506	2	2	2	x 50g balls
	♣	Black 302	4	4	4	x 50g balls
	▪	Smoke 339	4	4	4	x 50g balls

Children's Sweater Version 1

No.	Key	Colour	S	M	L	
Col 1	☐	Wine 307	4	4	4	x 50g balls
Col 2	☐	Slate 328	1	1	1	x 50g balls
Col 3	☐	Wine 307		(yarn already allowed for above)		
	+	Coral 304	1	1	1	x 50g balls
Col 4	⌂	Cherry 309	2	2	3	x 50g balls
	◊	Gold 320	1	1	1	x 50g balls
	■	Ginger 322	1	1	1	x 50g balls
	♣	Leaf 310	1	2	2	x 50g balls
	▪	Indigo 305	1	2	2	x 50g balls

Children's Sweater Version 2

No.	Key	Colour	S	M	L	
Col 1	☐	Violet 319	3	3	4	x 50g balls
Col 2	☐	Daisy 315	1	2	2	x 50g balls
Col 3	☐	Forest 318	1	1	1	x 50g balls
	+	Citrus 509	1	1	1	x 50g balls
	⌂	Mosaic 336	2	2	2	x 50g balls
	◊	Jacaranda 314	1	1	1	x 50g balls
	■	Avocado 337	1	1	1	x 50g balls
	♣	Jade 316	2	2	3	x 50g balls
Col 4	▪	Wedgewood 340	3	3	3	x 50g balls

NEEDLES

1 pair 3.75mm (UK 9) (USA 5)
1 pair 4.00mm (UK 8) (USA 6)
(adult) 1 x 3.25mm circular needle for neckband
(child) 1 x 3.75mm circular needle for neckband
1 Stitch holder

Harmony continued . . .

CHILDREN'S SWEATER
BACK
Using 3.75mm needles and Col 1, cast on 96(104,112)sts, then joining in Col 4, work in K2 P2 two Col rib as follows:
Row 1 (RS)[K2 Col 4, P2 Col 1) rep to end.
Row 2 (WS)[K2 Col 1, P2 Col 4] rep to end.
Rep these 2 rows 6 times (14 rows in all).
Change to 4.00mm needles and using st st, beg with a K row, foll graph for Col changes. Work this 74 row patt rep throughout. * Work 108(120,130)rows *(adjust length here if desired)*.
Cast off.

FRONT
Work as given for Back to *. Work 92(104,114)rows *(adjust length here if desired)*.
Shape front neck Keeping patt correct, work 39(43,47)sts, turn and leave rem sts on a st holder. Work each side of neck separately.
Cast off 2 sts at beg of next row, then 1 st at neck edge on foll rows, 8 times [29(33,37)sts]. Work 6 rows [108(120,130)rows].
Cast off.
With RS facing, leave 18 sts on a st holder, rejoin yarn to rem sts and complete second side to match first side, rev all shaping.

SLEEVES
Using 3.75 mm needles and Col 1, cast on 36(40,44) sts. Work in two colour rib as for back for 12 rows, inc 6(6,6)sts evenly across last row [42(46,50)sts].
Change to 4.00mm needles and using st st, beg with a K row, foll graph for Col changes. Work this 74 row patt rep throughout AT THE SAME TIME shape sides by inc 1 st at each end of 5th row, then 1 st each end of foll 4th rows, 14(16,19)times [72,(80,90)sts]. Work 9(7,5) rows [70(76,86)rows] *(adjust length here, if desired)*. Cast off loosely and evenly.

MAKING UP
Work as for Men's/Women's Sweater Back Making Up to **.
Neckband With RS facing, using 3.75mm circular needle and Col 1, pick up and K 20 sts down left side front neck, 18 sts from st holder across front neck, 20 sts up right side front neck and 38 sts across back of neck [96 sts]. Work in rounds in 2 Col rib as for adult's sweater for 3.5cm, inc 8 sts evenly across 1st row(104)sts. Cast off evenly in rib using Col 1. Press seams.

Harmony Child's Sweater, Version 1

Harmony Child's Sweater, Version 2 (right)

Lorikeet

Lorikeet, Version 2 (left)

L O R I K E E T

Knitting Rating: Average Skilled.
A lacey textured drop shoulder sweater knitted in a single colour or with 3 colour striped fabric.

MEASUREMENTS

Sizes	S	(M	L)	
To fit bust	80	90	100	cm
Bodice circumference	94	106	118	cm
Bodice length	66	66	66	cm
Sleeve length	47	47	47	cm

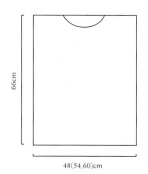

46(48,49.5)cm

47cm

66cm

48(54,60)cm

REQUIREMENTS

YARN
Jo Sharp 8 ply DK Pure Wool Hand Knitting Yarn.

No.	Colour		Yarn quantity		
Sizes		S	(M	L)	
Version 1					
Col 1	Jade 316	5	6	6	x 50g balls
Col 2	Mosaic 336	5	6	6	x 50g balls
Col 3	Aegean 504	5	6	6	x 50g balls
Version 2					
Col 1	Lichen 803	15	16	17	x 50g balls

NEEDLES
1 pair 3.75mm (USA 5) (UK 9)
1 pair 3.25mm (USA 3)(UK 10)
1 stitch holder

PATTERNS

TENSION
22.5 sts and 33 rows to 10cm, measured over Lacey Pattern, using 3.75mm needles.

SPECIAL ABBREVIATIONS
yrn - yarn round needle
yrn between two K sts - yarn forward as if to purl, then over needle to back of work.
yrn between two P sts - yarn over needle and then forward.
yrn between a K and a P st - yarn forward as if to purl, then over needle and forward.

Lorikeet, Version 1 (left)

LACEY PATTERN REPEAT
Row 1 * K1, P1, K1, (yrn, K2 tog through back of stitch) 2 times. Rep from * to last 3 sts K1, P1. K1.
Row 2 * K1, P1, K1, (yrn P2 tog)2 times. Rep from * to last 3 sts K1, P1, K1.

COLOUR SEQUENCE
*Rows 1 to 6 Col 1 / Rows 7 to 12 Col 2
Rows 13 to 18 Col 3 / Rep from * throughout.

LACEY TUNICS
BACK
Using 3.75mm needles and Col 1, cast on 108(122,136)sts.
Working Colour Sequence
(*above*) for Version 1 or using with Col 1 throughout for Version 2 and with Lacey Pattern (*as above*)
throughout, * work 218 rows (*adjust length here, if desired*).
Cast off.

FRONT
Work as given for Back to * work 190 rows (*adjust length here, if desired*).
Shape front neck Patt 47(54,61) turn and leave rem sts on a st holder.
Keeping patt correct, work each side of neck separately. Cast dec 1 st at neck edge on next 4 rows and then the foll 3rd row, 5 times [38(45,52)sts]. Patt 8 rows. Cast off. With RS facing, leave 14 sts on a st holder, rejoin yarn to rem sts. Work one row in patt. Complete second side to match first side.

SLEEVES
Using 3.75mm needles and Col 1, cast on 42(42,42)sts. Using Colour Sequence for Version 1 or Col 1 throughout for Version 2 and Lacey Pattern throughout, work 20 rows. Keeping patt correct, inc 1 st at each end of next row, then 1 st at each end of every foll 3rd row, 15(18,22)times [74(80,88)sts]. Then every 5th row, 15(14,12)times [104(108,112)sts]. Patt 13(9,7)rows straight 154 rows (*adjust length here, if desired*).
Cast off loosely and evenly.

MAKING UP
(*Note, use Col 1 throughout for version 2*)
Using backstitch, join right shoulder seam.
Neckband With RS facing, using 3.25mm needle and col 3, pick up and knit 26 sts down left side front neck, 14 sts from st holder at centre front, 26 sts up right side front neck and 32 sts across back neck (98 sts).
Work in Patt as follows:
Row 1 K1*yrn, K2 tog through back of st, rep from * to last st, K1.
Row 2 K1*yrn, P2 tog, rep from * to last st K1.
Rep rows 1 & 2 twice and Row 1, once.
Change to Col 2, rep row 2. Rep row 1 & 2.
Next row, knit. Cast off purlwise loosely and evenly.
The finished fabric should sit fairly flat.
If finished pieces are strongly ridged, press lightly with a damp cloth to achieve desired result.
Using backstitch join left shoulder seam, centre sleeves and join, join side and sleeve seams.

Thornbill

Thornbill Cardigan

Thornbill, Version 2 (left)

Thornbill Vest, Version 1

THORNBILL

Knitting Rating: Average with Cable knitting experience.
An elegant medium buttoning vest or cardigan with Cabled "v"-neck and Stocking stitch rolled edgings

MEASUREMENTS

Size	S	(M	L)	
To fit bust	80	90	100	cm
Bodice circumference	96	106	116	cm
Bodice length	65	66	67	cm
Sleeve length	43	43	43	cm

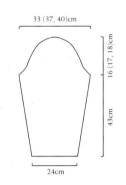

REQUIREMENTS

YARN

Jo Sharp 8 ply DK Pure Wool Hand Knitting Yarn

	Colour	Yarn Quantity			
Sizes		S	(M	L)	
Vest					
Version 1	Heron 802	12	13	14	x 50g balls
Version 2	Embers 804	12	13	14	x 50g balls
Cardigan	Chartreuse 330	17	17	18	x 50g balls

NEEDLES

1 pair 3.25mm (UK 10) (USA 3)
1 pair 4.00mm (UK 8) (USA 6)
A cable needle

BUTTONS

Vest or Cardigan - 6 x 1.5cm diameter.

PATTERNS

TENSION

32 sts and 30 rows to 10cm, measured over patt, using 4.00mm needles.

SPECIAL ABBREVIATIONS

Tw8rib - slip next 4 sts onto cable needle and leave at front of work, (K1tbl, P1) twice from left-hand needle, then (K1tbl, P1) twice from cable needle.

VEST
BACK

Using 3.25mm needles, cast on 159(175,191)sts.
Change to 4.00mm needles.
Beg patt.
Row 1 (P5,K1,P2), 0(1,0)time/s, P1, * K1, P2, (K1tbl,P1) 4 times, P1, K1, P3, rep from * to last 14(6,14)sts, K1, P2(5,2), [(K1tbl,P1) 4 times, P1, K1, P1] 1(0,1)time/s.
Row 2 K all the K sts and P all the P sts, as they face you.
Rep rows 1 and 2 twice.
Row 7 (P5,K1,P2) 0(1,0)time/s, P1, * K1, P2, Tw8rib, P1, K1, P3, rep from * to last 14(6,14)sts, K1, P2 (5,2), (Tw8rib,P1,K1, P1) 1(0,1)time/s.
Row 8 As row 2.
Rep rows 1 and 2 twice.
Rep these 12 rows for patt.
Cont in patt until work measures 42 cm from beg, ending with a WS row.
Shape armholes Keeping patt correct, cast off 9(11,13)sts at beg of next 2 rows [141(153,165)sts]. **
Dec 1 st at each end of next and alt rows 9(11,13)times [123(131,139)sts]. Work 47 rows.
Shape shoulders Cast off 10(11,11)sts at beg of next 6 rows, then 11(10,12)sts at beg of foll 2 rows. Cast off rem 41(45,49)sts.

LEFT FRONT

Using 3.25mm needles, cast on 79(87,95)sts.
Change to 4.00mm needles.
Beg patt.
Row 1 (P5,K1,P2) 0(1,0)time/s, P1, * K1, P2, (K1tbl,P1) 4 times, P1, K1, P3, rep from * to last 14 sts, K1, P2, (K1tbl,P1) 4 times, P1, K1, P1.
Row 2 K all the K sts and P all the P sts, as they face you.
Rep rows 1 and 2 twice.
Row 7 (P5,K1,P2) 0(1, 0)time/s, P1, * K1, P2, Tw8rib, P1, K1, P3, rep from * to last 14 sts, K1, P2, Tw8rib, P1, K1, P1.
Row 8 As row 2.
Rep rows 1 and 2 twice.
Rep these 12 rows for patt.
Cont in patt until work measures same as Back to armholes, ending with same patt row.
Shape armhole and front slope Keeping patt correct, cast off 9(11,13)sts at beg of next row [70 (76, 82)sts]. Work 1 row. Dec 1 st at each end of next and alt rows 9(11,13)times [52(54,56)sts], then at front edge only in foll 4th rows 11 times [41(43,45)sts]. Work 3 rows.
Shape shoulder Cast off 10(11,11)sts at beg of next and foll alt rows, 3 times. Work 1 row. Cast off rem 11(10,12)sts.

Thornbill continued . . .

RIGHT FRONT

Using 3.25mm needles, cast on 79(87,95)sts.
Change to 4.00mm needles.
Beg patt.
Row 1 P1, * K1, P2, (K1tbl,P1) 4 times, P1, K1, P3, rep from * to last 14(6,14)sts, K1, P2 (5,2), [(K1tbl,P1) 4 times, P1, K1, P1] 1 (0,1)time/s.
Row 2 K all the K sts and P all the P sts, as they face you.
Rep rows 1 and 2 twice.
Row 7 P1, * K1, P2, Tw8rib, P1, K1, P3, rep from * to last 14(6,14)sts, K1, P2 (5,2), (Tw8rib,P1,K1,P1), 1(0,1)time/s.
Row 8 As row 2.
Rep rows 1 and 2 twice.
Rep these 12 rows for patt.
Complete as for Left Front, keeping patt correct as placed in last 12 rows and rev all shaping.

MAKING UP

Press all pieces, very gently on WS using a warm iron over a damp cloth, taking care not to flatten patt. Using Backstitch, join shoulder seams.
Buttonhole Band With RS facing and using 3.25mm needles, pick up and K 93 sts evenly along Right Front edge to beg of front edge shaping, 68(72,76)sts evenly along shaped edge to shoulder and 15(17,19)sts evenly across half of back neck [176(182,188)sts]. Work 3 rows K1, P1 rib.
Row 4 Rib 4, * cast off 2 sts, rib 15, rep from * 4 times, cast off 2 sts, rib to end.
Row 5 Rib to last 79 sts * turn, cast on 2 sts turn, rib 15, rep from * 4 times turn, cast on 2 sts turn, rib 4 (6 buttonholes).
Work 2 rows rib, then 6 rows st st beg with a knit row. Cast off evenly.
Button Band Work to correspond with Buttonhole Band, omitting buttonholes.
Armhole Bands With RS facing, and using 3.25mm needles, pick up and K 128(140,152)sts evenly along armhole edge.
Work 7 rows K1 P1 rib. Work 6 rows st st. Cast off loosely and evenly.
Using Backstitch, join side and armhole band seams, rev seam on 6 st st rows on armhole bands. Join front bands at centre back neck, rev seam on 6 st st rows. Sew on buttons to correspond with buttonholes. Press seams.

CARDIGAN
BACK & FRONTS
Work as for Vest.

SLEEVES

Using 3.25mm needles, cast on 79 sts. Work 12 rows patt as for 1st Size of Back of Vest.
Change to 4.00mm needles.
Keeping patt correct as placed in last 12 rows and noting to work extra sts into patt, inc 1 st at each end of next row, then 1 st at each end of foll 6th(4th,4th)row, 2(10,22)times [85(101,125)sts], then every foll 8th(6th,6th)row, 11(10,2)times [107(121,129)sts]. Cont in patt without further shaping until work measures approx 43 cm (or length desired) from beg, ending with same patt row as Back and Front to armholes.
Shape top Keeping patt correct, cast off 5(6,7)sts at beg of next 2 rows [97(109,115)sts]. Dec 1 st at each end of next and alt rows 9(5,6)times [79(99,103)sts], then in every row 29(39,41)times [21 sts]. Cast off.

MAKING UP

Complete as for Vest omitting armhole bands. Sew in sleeves & join sleeve seams.

Thornbill Vest, Version 2

Thornbill Cardigan (right)

Tinglewood

TINGLEWOOD

Knitting Rating: Beginner.
This comfortable textured tunic has drop shoulder shaping and uses a simply worked four stitch Garter Rib throughout.
The women's version features side openings on the lower bodice.

MEASUREMENTS

Sizes	WOMEN'S			MEN'S			
	S	(M	L	S	M	L)	
	A	B	C	D	E	F	
To fit bust/chest	80	90	100	95	105	115	cm
Bodice circumference	101	108	116	116	124	131	cm
Bodice length	72	72	72	73	73	73	cm
Sleeve length	41	41	41	48	48	48	cm

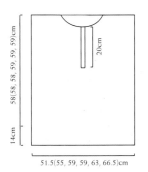
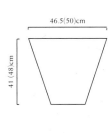

REQUIREMENTS

YARN
Jo Sharp 8 ply DK Pure Wool Hand Knitting Yarn.

Colour	Yarn Quantity			
Sizes	S	M	L	
Women's Tunic				
Hull 705	17	18	19	x 50g balls
Men's Tunic				
Heron 802	21	22	23	x 50g balls

NEEDLES
1 pair 3.75 mm (UK 9) (USA 5)
1 stitch holder

BUTTONS
4 x 1.5 cm diameter.

See page 27 for Men's Cap Pattern (left)

PATTERNS

TENSION
21 sts and 41 rows to 10cm, measured over Textured Pattern, using 3.75mm Needles.

TEXTURE PATTERN
All rows: *K4, P4, rep from * to end. This forms pattern throughout.

SWEATERS
BACK
Using 3.75mm needles, cast on 108(116,124,124,132,140)sts. Work in Textured Pattern* for 294(294,294,298,298,298)rows.
Shape Shoulders Cast off 8(9,10,10,11,11)sts at beg of next 10(8,4,4,2,8)rows, then 0(8,9,9,10,10)sts at beg of foll rows 0(2,6,6,8,2)times. Cast off rem 28(28,30,30,30,32)sts.

FRONT
Work as given for back to*.
Work 184(180,176,181,177,173)rows.
Divide for button opening (*Womens RS facing, Men's WS facing*)
Row 1 Patt 51(55,59,59,63,67)sts, K6, turn and leave rem sts on a stitch holder.
Row 2 K6, patt to end.
Work a further 81 rows on these sts keeping patt and border correct 267(263,259,264,260,256)rows.
Shape front neck for women's sizes WS facing, for men's sizes RS facing, cast off 8 sts at beg of next row. Patt to end [49(53,57,57,61,65)sts]. Keeping patt correct dec 1 st at neck edge on next and alt rows 6(5,6,5,5,5)times, then every 3rd row 3(4,2,3,3,3)times, then every 4th row 0(0,2,2,2,3)times [40(44,47,47,51,54)sts]. Work 6(9,9,9,11,11)rows without shaping.
Shape shoulders Cast off 8(9,10,10,11,11)sts at beg of next and every alt row 5(4,2,2,1,4)times, then 0(8,9,9,10,10)sts, 0(1,3,3,4,1)times.
(*With RS facing for Women's and WS facing for Men's*) Pick up sts from stitch holder, rejoin yarn at neck edge, and cast on extra 6 sts. Work as for left/right side, rev all shaping AT THE SAME TIME making 4 button holes spaced evenly between, the first to come 2 cm from bottom edge of opening, the last to come 1cm from top of neck opening as follows:
Row 1 K2, cast off 2, K2, patt to end.
Row 2 Patt to last 2 sts turn, cast on 2 turn, K2.

SLEEVES
note: Mens sleeve shown in ( ).
Using 3.75 needles, cast on 52(60)sts. Work in textured patt for 14 rows, keeping patt correct. Inc 1 st at each end of next row, then every foll 6th(7th)row, 22 times [155(183)rows] [98(106sts]. Work 22(28)rows, or until length desired [169(197)rows]. Cast off loosely and evenly.

MAKING UP
Using Backstitch, join shoulder seams. Centre sleeves and join, join side and sleeve seams, leaving 14cm open on sides. Sew buttonhole flap into place to overlap the button band, sew on buttons to correspond with buttonholes. Press seams only.

TRUE

Knitting Rating: Average skilled.
This drop shoulder tunic features a knitted lace border on sleeves, bodice and collar.
A knit and purl repeat pattern is worked throughout to create the elegantly textured surface design.

MEASUREMENTS

Women's Tunic

Sizes	S	(M	L)
To fit bust	80	90	100
Bodice circumference	116	122	128
Bodice Length	66	67	68
Sleeve length	41	41	41

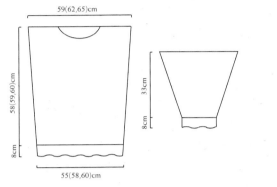

Girl's Sweater

Sizes	4-6	8-10
To fit chest	60	70
Bodice circumference	76	88
Bodice length	41	48
Sleeve length	30	36

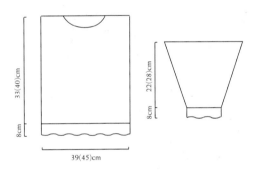

REQUIREMENTS

YARN

Jo Sharp 8 ply DK Pure Wool Hand Knitting Yarn

	Colour	Quantity			
Sizes		S	(M	L)	
Women's	Lilac 324	14	14	15	x50g balls
Sizes		4-6yo	(8-10yo)		
Child's	Jade 316	7	9		x 50g balls

NEEDLES

1 pair 4.00mm (UK 8) (USA 6)

PATTERNS

TENSION

22 sts and 32 rows to 10cm measured over pattern using 4.00mm needles.

WOMEN'S TUNIC
BACK

Using 4.00mm needles, cast on 121(127,133)sts.
Foll graph for 26 row patt rep, work in patt inc 1 st at each end of 27th row, then 1 st each end of foll 26th rows 4 times, noting to work the extra sts made into the pattern.
Cont on these 131(137,143)sts until work measures 58(59,60)cm (*or desired length*) from beg (*noting that edging measures approx 8cm*) ending with a WS row.
Shape back neck Patt 49(52,55), cast off next 33 sts loosely, patt to end.
Cont on last 49(52,55)sts and keeping patt correct, dec 1 st at neck edge in next 4 rows [45(48,51)sts].
Shape shoulder Cast off 10(11,12)sts at beg of next and foll alt rows 3 times in all, AT THE SAME TIME dec 1 st at neck edge in every row 4 times. Work 1 row. Cast off rem 11 sts.
With WS facing, rejoin yarn to rem sts and complete second side to match first side, rev all shaping.

Chapter 4
The Locals Call It The Lake

Edward Proctor, became part of the Rudgyard Story when he married Olive Harrison, daughter of Paul and Sarah Harrison.

In his later years, Edward wrote down the story of Rudgyard, beginning with the early pioneering days when farming was a struggle and due to the inherently poor soil, neither crops nor cattle could survive. In the late forties, Edward solved the soil deficiency problem, and with the help of his son Ron, successful pastures were grown and healthy stock raised.

Edward also established a modest holiday resort which supplemented farm income. The Wilson Inlet is called "The Lake" by locals and fishing has always been a part of the Rudgyard lifestyle. For many years a vessel called "The Little True" was used by the family to fish and take holiday makers for pleasure cruises.

Edward's daughter Beryl loved fishing, and when she wasn't helping to run the holiday cottages she went out with her father on "The Little True". Eventually, Beryl's brother Ron and his wife Jess took on the cottages, leaving Beryl free to fish. Ron and Jess have since given up the resort, however still live on the farm, and Ron still fishes and now breeds ostriches. These days, Beryl helps her sons with the fishing, that's when she's not indulging in her other love of collecting elephant art. At last count she had collected 1,535 elephant artifacts!

The story having been told . . . Rudgyard Beach now awaits the next generation to discover it's timeless treasures.

Wattletop

Men's Vest (left), Women's Cropped Sweater (right)

Page opposite, from top left clockwise
Child's Cardigan, Men's Sweater,
Women's Cropped Cardigan, Child's Sweater.

WATTLETOP

Knitting Rating: Average with Fairisle skill.
This classic Fairisle pattern is featured in styles and sizes for adults and children.
The Adult patterns are a classic and close fit and the children's are loose fitting drop shoulder style.

MEASUREMENTS

Note: Each version (cardigan, sweater, vest etc.) gives a pattern for all sizes and sexes, however this book shows just one unique colourway for each style given, either as a Men's Women's or Child's garment.

Adult's

Sizes	WOMENS			MENS			
	S	(M	L	S	M	L)	
	A	B	C	D	E	F	
To fit bust/chest	80	90	100	95	105	115	cm
Bodice circumference	98	111	120	116	125	135	cm
Bodice length	66	68	69	70	72	72.5	cm
Bodice length / cropped	51	53	54	55	57	57.5	cm
Sleeve length	42	42	42	49	49	49	cm

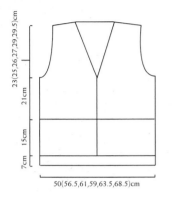

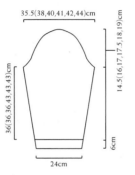

Children's

Sizes	3-4yo	(5-6 yo	7-8yo)	
To fit chest	60	65	70	cm
Bodice circumference	83	88	92	cm
Bodice length	39	43	47	cm
Sleeve length	26	32	37	cm

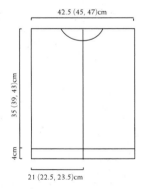

Women's Cropped Cardigan (left)

REQUIREMENTS

NEEDLES

1 pair 3.25mm (UK 10) (USA 3)
1 pair 3.75mm needles (UK 9) (USA.5)
1 x 3.75mm circular needle(UK 9)(USA.5) *(child's sweater only)*
1 pair 4.50mm (UK 7) (USA 7)
2 Stitch Holders for Sweater or Cardigan

BUTTONS

Women's Cropped Cardigan - 5 x 1.5cm
Wom. & Men's Classic Cardigan 7 x 1.5cm *(not illustrated)*
Children's Cardigan - 4 x 1.5cm

YARN

Note: Volumes given only for illustrated versions.
Jo Sharp 8 ply DK Pure Wool Hand Knitting Yarn.

No.	Key	Colour	Yarn Quantities						
Sizes			A	B	C	D	E	F	

Men's Sweater

No.	Key	Colour	A	B	C	D	E	F	
1	☐	Smoke 339	8	8	9	9	10	10	x 50g balls
2	+	Heron 802	2	3	4	4	4	5	x 50g balls
	∩	Antique 323	3	3	3	3	4	4	x 50g balls
	▪	Jade 316	1	2	2	2	2	2	x 50g balls
	■	Miro 507	2	2	2	2	2	3	x 50g balls

Women's Cropped Sweater

No.	Key	Colour	A	B	C	D	E	F	
1	☐	Heron 802	6	7	7	7	8	8	x 50g balls
	+	Miro 507	2	3	3	3	3	4	x 50g balls
2	∩	Antique 323	2	3	3	3	3	4	x 50g balls
	▪	Jade 316	1	2	2	2	2	2	x 50g balls
	■	Wine 307	1	2	2	2	2	2	x 50g balls

Men's Vest

No.	Key	Colour	A	B	C	D	E	F	
1	☐	Jade 316	6	6	6	7	7	7	x 50g balls
2	+	Wine 307	2	2	2	3	3	3	x 50g balls
	∩	Antique 323	2	2	2	2	3	3	x 50g balls
	▪	Heron 802	1	1	1	1	2	2	x 50g balls
	■	Miro 507	1	1	1	1	2	2	x 50g balls

Women's Cropped Cardigan

No.	Key	Colour	A	B	C	D	E	F	
1	☐	Ruby 326	6	6	6	6	7	7	x 50g balls
2	+	Citrus 509	4	4	4	4	4	5	x 50g balls
3	∩	Avocado 337	2	2	3	3	3	3	x 50g balls
	▪	Jade 316	1	2	2	2	2	2	x 50g balls
4	■	Aegean 504	2	2	2	2	3	3	x 50g balls

Sizes			3-4 yo	(5-6 yo	7-8yo)	

Child's Sweater

No.	Key	Colour	3-4 yo	(5-6 yo	7-8yo)	
1	☐	Heron 802	5	5	5	x 50g balls
2	+	Earth 334	3	3	4	x 50g balls
	∩	Antique 323	2	2	2	x 50g balls
	▪	Ginger 322	1	1	1	x 50g balls
	■	Chestnut 506	1	1	2	x 50g balls

Child's Cardigan

No.	Key	Colour	3-4 yo	(5-6 yo	7-8yo)	
1	☐	Owl 801	4	4	4	x 50g balls
	+	Antique 323	3	3	3	x 50g balls
	∩	Citrus 509	2	2	2	x 50g balls
	▪	Ruby 326	1	1	1	x 50g balls
	■	Jade 316	1	1	1	x 50g balls

WATTLETOP
FRONT, BACK AND SLEEVES

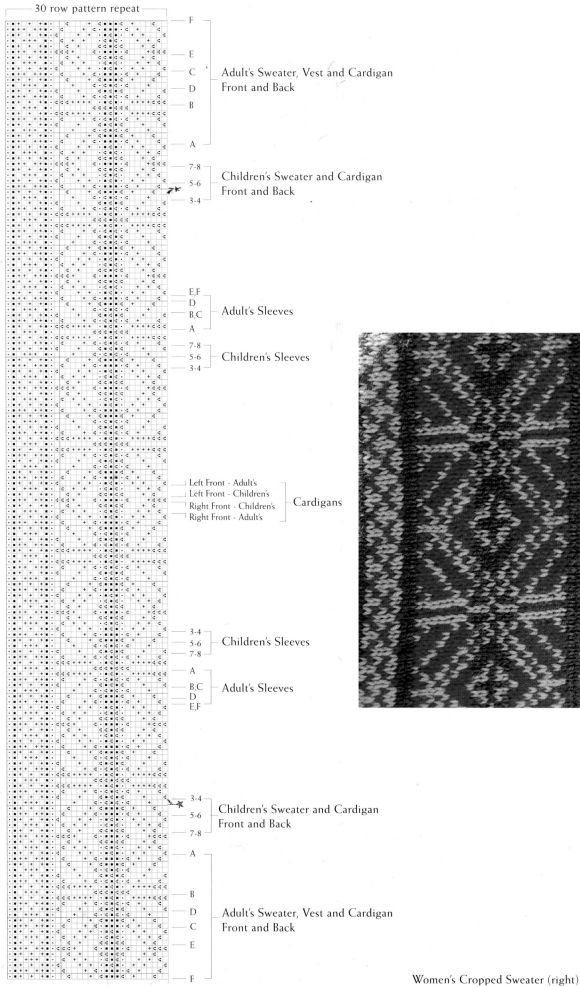

30 row pattern repeat

F
E
C — Adult's Sweater, Vest and Cardigan
D   Front and Back
B
A

7-8
5-6 — Children's Sweater and Cardigan
3-4   Front and Back

E,F
D
B,C — Adult's Sleeves
A

7-8
5-6 — Children's Sleeves
3-4

Left Front - Adult's
Left Front - Children's
Right Front - Children's — Cardigans
Right Front - Adult's

3-4
5-6 — Children's Sleeves
7-8

A
B,C — Adult's Sleeves
D
E,F

3-4
5-6 — Children's Sweater and Cardigan
7-8   Front and Back

A

B

D — Adult's Sweater, Vest and Cardigan
C   Front and Back

E

F

Women's Cropped Sweater (right)

78

Wattletop Men's Sweater

Wattletop continued . . .
PATTERNS
TENSION
25 sts and 25 rows to 10cm, measured over Fairisle, using 4.50mm needles.

MEN'S SWEATER & WOMEN'S CROPPED SWEATER
BACK
Using 3.25mm needles and Col 1, cast on 113(127,139,133,145,157)sts.
Row 1 K2, * P1, K1, rep from * to last st, K1.
Row 2 K1, * P1, K1, rep from * to end.
Change to Col 2 and rep these 2 rows once. Change to Col 1 and rep these 2 rows 10 times, inc 14 sts evenly across last row. [127(141,153,147,159,171)sts, 24 rows rib in all]
Change to 4.50mm needles. Rows 1 to 30 incl from graph form patt. Rep this patt until 90 rows worked for the men's classic version, or 52 rows for the women's cropped version.
Shape armholes Keeping patt correct, cast off 9(12,13,10,12,14)sts at beg of next 2 rows [109(117,127,127,135,143)sts] ***
Dec 1 st at each end of every row 9(11,13,10,11,13)times [91(95,101,107,113,117)sts]. Work 41(43,43,50,53,53)rows patt.
Shape shoulders Cast off 9(10,10,11,12,12)sts at beg of next 4 rows, then 10(9,11,11,11,12)sts at beg of foll 2 rows. Cast off rem 35(37,39,41,43,45)sts.

FRONT
Work as for given for Back to ***
Divide for "V" neck Next row K2tog, patt 52(56,61,61,65,69), turn. Cont on these 53(57,62,62,66,70)sts.
Dec 1 st at armhole edge in every row 8(10,12,9,10,12)times, AT THE SAME TIME dec 1 st at neck edge in alt rows 11(11,12,12,12,13)times [34(36,38,41,44,45)sts], then in foll 4th rows 6(7,7,8,9,9)times [28(29,31,33,35,36)sts]. Work three rows.
Shape shoulder Cast off 9(10,10,11,12,12)sts at beg of next row and foll alt row. Work 1 row. Cast off rem 10(9,11,11,11,12)sts.
With RS facing, slip next st onto a thread and leave, rejoin yarn to rem sts and complete second side to match first side, rev all shaping.

SLEEVES
Using 3.25mm needles and Col 1, cast on 47(53,53,57,59,59)sts.
Work 20 rows of rib as for back, omitting colour change and inc 14 sts evenly across last row [61(67,67,71,73,73)sts].
Change to 4.50mm needles. Cont in patt as for Back placing patt from diagram and keeping patt correct shape sides by inc 1 st at each end of 5th row, then 1 st at each end of every foll 4th row 3(3,12,1,1,10)times [69(75,93,75,77,95)sts], then every foll 6th row 10(10,4,14,14,8)times [89(95,101,103,105,111)sts]. Work 13(13,13,15,15,15)rows patt, [90(90,90,108,108,108)rows in all].
Shape top Keeping patt correct, cast off 5(6,7,5,6,7)sts at beg of next 2 rows [79(83,87,93,93,97)sts].
Dec 1 st at each end of next and alt rows 6(8,8,7,9,9)times [67(67,71,79,75,79)sts], then in every row 23(23,25,29,27,29)times [21 sts]. Cast off.

MAKING UP
Press all pieces, gently on WS using a warm iron over a damp cloth. Using Backstitch, join right shoulder seam.
Neckband With RS facing, using 3.25mm needles and Col 1, pick up and K 60(62,64,70,74,76)sts evenly along left side of front neck, K st from thread (centre st), pick up and K 60(62,64,70,74,76)sts evenly along right side of front neck, then pick up and K 35(37,39,41,43,45)sts across back of neck. [156(162,168,182,192,198)sts].
Row 1 * K1, P1, rep from * to end.
Row 2 Rib to within 2 sts of centre st, yb, sl1, K1, psso, K1 (centre st), K2tog, rib to end.
Row 3 Rib to within 2 sts of centre st, K2tog, P1, K2tog tbl, rib to end.
Rep 2nd and 3rd rows, 4 times [11 rows rib in all].
Cast off in rib. Using Backstitch, join left shoulder and neckband seam. *** Join side and sleeve seams. Sew in sleeves. Press seams.

MEN'S VEST (above)
(women's sizes also given)
BACK
Work as given for Back of Sweater.

FRONT
Work as given for Front of Sweater.

MAKING UP
Work as given for Sweater Making Up to ***.
Armhole Bands With RS facing, using 3.25mm needles and Col 1, pick up and K 117(131,137,139,147,159)sts evenly along armhole edge. Working in rib as for sweater back, work 2 rows Col 1, 2 rows Col 2, 7 rows Col 1, cast off loosely in rib.
Using Backstitch, join side and armhole band seams. Press seams.

Wattletop continued . . .
WOMEN'S CROPPED CARDIGAN
(Classic length and Men's sizes also given, however not illustrated)

BACK
Work as given for Back of Sweater, omitting colour change in rib. Work 24 rows rib in all.

LEFT FRONT
Using 3.25mm needles and Col 1, Cast on 54(61,67,64,70,76)sts. Work 24 rows in rib as for Back of sweater (omitting colour change), inc 7sts evenly across last row 61(68,74,71,77,83)sts. Change to 4.50mm needles and rep patt from graph for 90 rows for classic version or 52 rows for cropped version.

Shape armholes Keeping patt correct, cast off 9(12,13,10,12,14)sts at beg of next row. Work 1row straight. Dec 1 st at armhole edge every row 9(11,13,10,11,13)times. 43(45,48,51,54,56)sts. Work 19(19,19,26,27,25)rows patt.

Shape front neck Next row Patt 36(38,40,42,45,47)sts and leave rem 7(7,8,9,9,9)sts on a stitch holder, turn. Dec 1 st at neck edge in alt rows 8(9,9,9,10,11)times [28(29,31,33,35,36)sts]. Work 5 rows.

Shape shoulder Cast off 9(10,10,11,12,12)sts at beg of next row and foll alt row. Work 1 row. Cast off rem 10(9,11,11,11,12)sts.

RIGHT FRONT
Work as for Left Front rev all shaping.

SLEEVES
Knit as for Sweater Sleeves using the following colour substitution;
Substitute Col 1 with Col 2 and visa versa throughout
Substitute Col 3 with Col 4 and visa versa throughout

MAKING UP
Press all pieces, gently on WS using a warm iron over a damp cloth. Using Backstitch, join shoulder seams. Centre sleeves and join. Join side and sleeve seams using edge to edge stitch on ribs. **

Neckband With RS facing, using 3.75mm needles and Col 1, pick up and K 7(7,8,9,9,9)sts from stitch holder, 28sts up right front, 44 sts across back neck, 28 sts down left front and 7(7,8,9,9,9)sts from stitch holder at left front. 114(115,116,116,116)sts. Work 8 rows K1 P1 rib, cast off evenly in rib.

Button Band *(note: rev bands for Men's cardigan)*
With RS facing, using 3.75mm needles and Col 1, pick up and K [for cropped version] 102(104,106,110,112,114)sts [for classic version] 140(142,144,148,150,150)sts evenly along front, from cast off edge of neckband to bottom edge. Work in 8 rows in K1 P1 rib. Cast off evenly in rib. Mark position on button band for 6 buttons *(or 7 buttons for classic version)* the first to come 2cm up from lower edge, the last to come 2cm from top edge, and the remainder spaced evenly between. Sew on buttons.

Button Hole Band Work as for button band, making button holes to correspond with position of buttons. Press seams.

Wattletop Continued . . .

CHILD'S SWEATER (below)

BACK
Using 3.75 mm needles and Col 1, cast on 107(113,119)sts. Work in K1, P1 rib as follows: 2 rows Col 1, 2 rows Col 2, 8 rows Col 1.
Change to 4.50mm needles and using st st, beg with a K row, ref to graph and 30 row patt rep for col changes and position of children's sizes. * Work 88(98,108)rows. Cast off.

FRONT
Work as given for Child's Back to *. Work 72(82,92)rows.
Shape front neck Work 44(47,50)sts, turn and leave rem sts on a holder. Work each side of neck separately. Cast off 2 sts at beg of next and foll row, and 1 st at neck edge of foll 10 rows [30(33,36)sts]. Work 3 rows. Cast off. With RS facing, leave 19 sts on a holder, rejoin yarn to rem sts and complete second side to match first side, rev all shaping.

SLEEVES
Using 3.75 mm needles and Col 2, cast on 40(44,48)sts. Work in K1, P1 rib for 14 rows inc 7(7,7)sts evenly across last (WS) row [47(51,55)sts].
Change to 4.50mm needles and refer to graph for sleeve position. Beg with a K row, foll 30 row patt rep, substituting Col 1 with Col 2 and visa versa throughout AT THE SAME TIME, shape sides by inc 1 st at each end of 7th(7th,6th)row, then 1 st at each end of every foll 3rd(4th,3rd)row 7(7,7)times, then every foll 3rd(3rd,4th)row, 8(10,12)times [79(87,95)sts]. Work 3(5,8)rows [55(70,83)rows]. Cast off loosely and evenly.

MAKING UP
Work as for Women's Cropped Cardigan "MAKING UP" to **.
Neckband Using 3.75mm circular needle or a set of 4, 3.75mm double pointed needles and Col 1, with RS facing, pick up and K18 sts down left side front neck, 19 sts from stitch holder across front neck, 18 sts up right side front neck and 45 sts across back of neck [100 sts]. Work in K1, P1 rib for 10 rounds. Cast off evenly in rib. Press seams.

CHILD'S CARDIGAN (left)

BACK
Work as for Child's Sweater Back, omitting colour change in rib and working 12 rows rib in all with Col 1.

LEFT FRONT
Using 3.75mm needles and Col 1, cast on 53(56,59)sts. Work in K1, P1 rib for 12 rows.
Change to 4.50mm needles and using st st, beg with a K row, ref to graph for col changes. Work 76(86,96)rows.
Shape front neck Work 44(47,50)sts, turn and leave rem 9 sts on a holder. Cast off 2 sts at beg of next row, then 1 st at neck edge of next 7 rows [35(38,41)sts]. Work 3 rows. Cast off.

RIGHT FRONT
Work as for Left Front, rev all shaping and foll Right Front Graph for Col changes.

SLEEVES
Work as for Child's Sweater Sleeves using Col 1 for rib and without substituting Col 1 with Col 2 and visa versa when following graph.

MAKING UP
Work as for Womens Cropped Cardigan "MAKING UP" to **.
Neckband With RS facing, using 3.75mm needles and Col 1, slip 9 sts from st holder on Right Front then pick up and knit 13 sts up Right Front, 36 sts across back neck, 13 sts down left front, and knit 9 sts from st holder on Left Front [80sts]. Work K1, P1 rib for 8 rows. Cast off evenly in rib.
Button Band With RS facing using 3.75mm needles and Col 1, pick up and knit K92(102,112)sts evenly along front from bottom edge to cast off edge of neckband of right front (for boy - for girl pick up from top to bottom of left front). Work in K1, P1 rib for 8 rows. Cast off evenly in rib. Mark position on button band for 5 buttons, the first to come 1 cm from lower edge, the last to come 1 cm from top edge and the remainder spaced evenly inbetween. Sew on buttons.
Button hole band Work as for button band, making button holes to correspond with position of buttons. Press seams.

Wingbeat

WINGBEAT

Knitting Rating: Experienced with Intarsia Knowledge.
This long line Jacket has Garter stitch collar & front bands, deep side seam pockets
and textured bands. The sleeves have fringes made from frayed wool yarn.

MEASUREMENTS

Sizes	S	(M	L)
To fit bust	80	90	100 cm
Bodice circumference	117	124	131 cm
Bodice length	71	71	71 cm
Sleeve length	39	39	39 cm

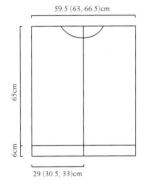

REQUIREMENTS

YARN

Jo Sharp 8 ply Pure Wool Hand Knitting Yarn.

No.	Key	Colour	Quantity			
Sizes			S	(M	L)	
Col 1	■	Owl 801	8	8	8	x 50g balls
Col 2	□	Slate 328	5	5	5	x 50g balls
Col 3	⊠	Ruby 326	2	2	2	x 50g balls
	▪	Avocado 337	2	2	2	x 50g balls
	◥	Forest 318	2	2	2	x 50g balls
	⋒	Antique 323	1	1	1	x 50g balls
	❖	Khaki 329	2	2	2	x 50g balls
	▣	Wine 307	1	1	1	x 50g balls

NEEDLES

1 pair 3.25mm (UK 10) (USA 3)
1 pair 4.00mm (UK 8) (USA 6)
2 stitch holders

BUTTONS

7 x 2.5cm diameter.

PATTERN

TENSION

22.5 sts and 30 rows to 10cm measured over Stocking stitch
using 4.00mm needles.

WOMEN'S JACKET

BACK

Using 3.25mm needles and Col 1, cast on 134(142,150)sts.
Work in textured rib for 22 rows as follows:
Row 1 (RS) K4(2,0),*P3 K1 P3 K3. Rep from * to end.
Row 2 * P3 K3 P1 K3. Rep from * to last 4(2,0)sts P4(2,0).
Row 3 As row 1.
Row 4 Knit.
Rep rows 1 to 4, 4 times, then rows 1 and 2 once (22 rows).
Change to 4.00mm needles and using St St, beg with a K row,
foll graph for Col changes.* Work 196 rows or until length
desired. Cast off.

LEFT FRONT

Using 3.25mm needles and Col 1, cast on 67(71,75)sts. Work
in textured rib for 22 rows as follows:
Row 1 (RS) K0(2,4)* P3 K1 P3 K3 rep from * to last 7(9,1)sts.
P3 K1 P3 (P3 K1 P3 K2, K1).
Row 2 K3 P1 K3 (P2 K3 P1 K3, P1) * P3 K3 P1 K3. Rep
from * to last 0(2,4)sts P 0(2,4).
Row 3 As row 1.
Row 4 Knit.
Rep rows 1 to 4, 4 times then rows 1 and 2 once (22 rows).
Change to 4.00mm needles and using st st, beg with a K row,
foll graph for Col changes. Work 166 rows.

WINGBEAT

SLEEVE

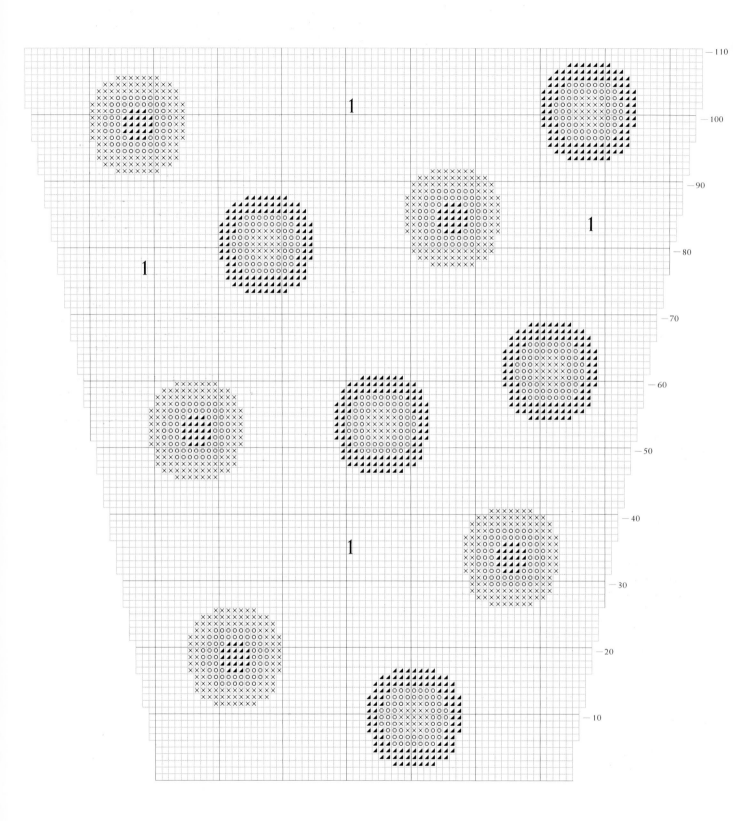

Wingbeat continued . . .

Shape front neck Work 55(59,63)sts, turn and leave rem 12 sts on a stitch holder. Cast off 2 sts at beg of next and foll alt rows, three times [49(53,57,)sts] then 1 st at neck edge of foll alt rows, 4 times [45(49,53)sts]. Work 16 rows. Cast off.

RIGHT FRONT
Using 3.25mm needles and Col 1, cast on 67(71,75)sts. Work as for Left Front, rev all shaping and foll graph for Col changes.

SLEEVES
Using 3.25mm needles and Col 1, cast on 65 sts. Work 10 rows in Garter st.

Change to 4.00mm needles and using St St, beg with a K row, foll graph for Col changes AT THE SAME TIME, shape sides by inc 1 st at each end of 7th row, then 1 st at each end of every foll 5th row, 19 times [105 sts]. Work 8 rows [110 rows]. Cast off loosely and evenly.

Make tassles on sleeves Thread a needle with two 15cm lengths of Col 3. With RS of sleeve facing, pass the needle through the fabric from front to back on one side of the centre stitch of the flower motif, then return needle to front of work on the other side of centre stitch. Knot ends to form tassle. Separate yarn into 16 single strands. Trim ends to 4.5cm. Rep for each flower motif.

POCKET LININGS (make 2)
Using 4.00mm needles and Col 2, cast on 33 sts. Using St st, work 60 rows. Cast off.

MAKING UP
Press all pieces, gently, on WS using a warm iron over a damp cloth. Using backstitch, join shoulder seams. Centre sleeves and join. Using Backstitch, join sleeve seams, using edge to edge st on cuffs.

Button Band With RS facing, using 3.25mm needles and Col 1, cast on 7 sts. Work in Garter st until band when slightly stretched is the same length as the Front, to beg of neck shaping. Sew band into position as you go. Leave the 7 sts on the stitch holder at neckline. Mark position on band for 7 buttons, the first to come 2cm from lower edge, the last to come at top of band, the other 5 spaced evenly between.

Button hole Band Work to correspond with Button Band, working 7 Button holes opposite markers as follows: K2, cast off 3, K2. On next row, cast on 3 sts in place of those cast off on previous row.

Neckband and Collar With RS facing, using 3.25mm needles, pick up 19 sts from stitch holder, 26 sts up Right Front neck, 44 sts across Back neck, 26 sts down Left Front neck and 19 sts from stitch Holder at Left Front neck (134 sts). Using Col 1, work 4 rows in Garter st. Cast off 4 sts at beg of next 2 rows. Work 4 more rows in Garter stitch (10 rows). Change to 4.00mm needles and work 16 rows in Garter st. Cast off.

Pockets Slip stitch RS of pocket linings to WS of Fronts on 3 sides, placing cast-on edge of lining to top of ribbing and 60 rows along side edge of Front, leaving this side edge open. Using backstitch, join side seams, stitching both pocket lining and Front to Back for 25 rows above ribbing, then pocket lining only to Back for next 35 rows, then Fronts to Back for remainder.

Pocket edgings With RS facing, using 3.25mm needles and Col 2, pick up 32 sts evenly along side edge (pocket) openings on Fronts. Knit 2 rows. Cast off.

Slip st side edge of pocket edgings into position, overlapping Back. Sew on buttons. Press seams.

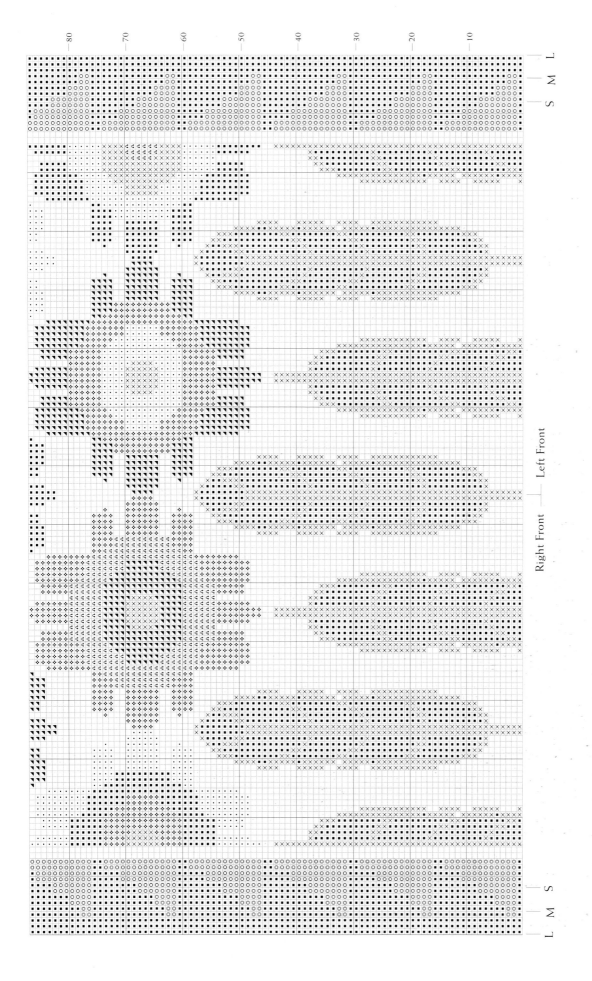

Right Front   Left Front

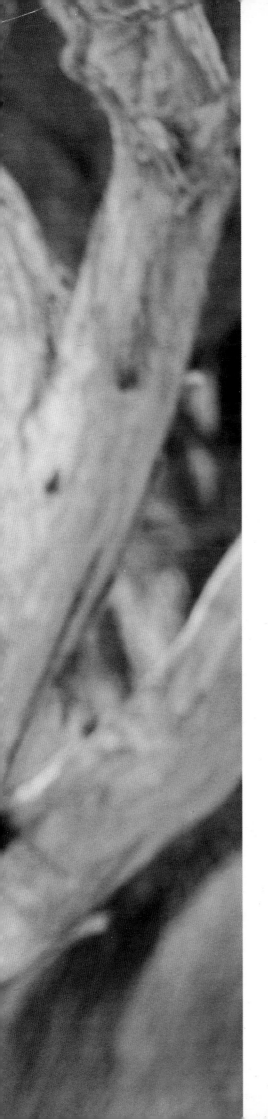

Woodswallow

WOODSWALLOW

Knitting Rating: Experienced with Fairisle knowledge.
A classic women's Raglan Jacket featuring shaped Fairisle collar, Fairisle bodice and sleeve borders,
deep side seam pockets and contrasting picot edgings.

MEASUREMENTS

Sizes	A	(B	C	D	E	F)
	XS	S	M	L	XL	XXL
To fit bust	75	80	85	90	95	100 cm
Bodice circumference	104	109	113	120	125	130 cm
Bodice length	70	71	71	72	72	73 cm
Sleeve seam length	41	41	41	41	41	41 cm

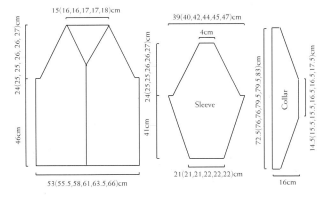

15(16,16,17,17,18)cm

39(40,42,44,45,47)cm

4cm

24(25,25,26,26,27)cm

24(25,25,26,26,27)cm

Sleeve

Collar

46cm

41cm

72.5(76,76,79.5,79.5,83)cm

14.5(15.5,15,15,16.5,17.5)cm

53(55.5,58,61,63.5,66)cm

21(21,21,22,22,22)cm

16cm

REQUIREMENTS

YARN

Jo Sharp 8 ply DK Pure Wool Hand Knitting Yarn.

No.	Key	Colour	Yarn Quantity					
Sizes			A	B	C	D	E	F
			XS	S	M	L	XL	XXL
1	☐	Owl 801	17	17	18	18	19	19 x 50g balls
2	☐▮	Violet 319	3	4	4	4	5	5 x 50g balls

NEEDLES

1 pair 3.25mm (UK 10) (USA 3)
1 pair 3.75mm (UK 9 (USA 5) (if nec. on rows 3 - 5 on front bands)
1 pair 4.00mm (UK 8) (USA 6)
1 pair 4.50mm (UK 7) (USA 7)(if necessary on fairisle)

BUTTONS

5 x 2.5cm diameter.

PATTERN

TENSION

22.5 sts and 30 rows to 10cm, measured over Stocking st, using
4.00mm Needles.

WOMEN'S JACKET

BACK

Using 3.25mm Needles and Col 1, cast on
119(125,131,137,143,149)sts.
Work 8 rows st st.
Next row (picot row) K1, * yf, K2tog, rep from * to end.
Next row Purl.
Change to 4.00mm needles (or 4.50mm if necessary to achieve correct
tension on Fairisle) and using st st (beg with a K row) foll graph A
for col changes for next 60 rows, then cont with Col 1 until
work measures 46cm from start of Graph A.
Shape raglan armholes Cast off 3 sts at beg of next 2 rows
[113(119,125,131,137,143)sts].
Dec 1 st at each end of next and alt rows
32(34,31,31,28,30)times in all [49(51,63,69,81,83)sts], then in
every row 7(7,13,15,21,21)times [35(37,37,39,39,41)sts].
Cast off.

LEFT FRONT

Using 3.25mm Needles and Col 1, cast on
59(61,65,67,71,73)sts. Work 8 rows st st.
Next row (picot row) K1, * yf, K2tog, rep from * to end.
Next row Purl, inc 0(1,0,1,0,1)st/s in centre of last row
[59(62,65,68,71,74)sts].
Change to 4.00mm Needles and using st st (beg with a K row)
foll graph A for col changes for 60 rows and continue using
Col 1 until work measures 46cm from start of Graph A. **
Shape raglan armhole Cast off 3 sts at beg of next row
[56(59,62,65,68,71)sts]. Work 1 row.
Dec 1 st at beg of next and alt rows 8 times in all
[48(51,54,57,60,63)sts]. Work 1 row.
Shape front slope Dec 1 st at each end of next and alt rows
5(5,5,6,6,6)times in all [38(41,44,45,48,51)sts].
Dec 1 st at armhole edge in alt rows 19(21,18,17,14,16)times,
then in every row 7(7,13,15,21,21)times, AT THE SAME TIME
dec 1 st at front edge in foll 4th rows 10(11,11,11,11,12)times
[2 sts].
Next row K2 tog. Fasten off.

RIGHT FRONT

Work as for Left Front to **. Work 1 row.
Shape raglan armhole Cast off 3 sts at beg of next row
[56(59,62,65,68,71)sts].
Dec 1 st at end of next and alt rows 8 times in all
[48(51,54,57,60,63)sts]. Work 1 row.
Shape front slope Complete to correspond with Left Front.

WOODSWALLOW

FRONT, BACK AND SLEEVES
(GRAPH A)

WOODSWALLOW
COLLAR AND BANDS
(GRAPH B)

F

D-E

B-C

A

Button, Buttonhole band
All sizes

Button, Buttonhole band
All sizes

A

B-C

D-E

F

SLEEVES

Using 3.25mm Needles and Col 1, cast on
49(51,51,53,53,55)sts. Work 8 rows st st.
Next row (picot row) K1, * yf, K2tog, rep from * to end.
Next row Purl.
Change to 4.00mm Needles, using st st (beg with a K row), foll
graph A for col changes & sleeve positioning work 8 rows
straight. Cont foll graph for col changes for next 52 rows then
cont in Col 1 for remainder of sleeve, AT THE SAME TIME
shape sides by inc 1 st at each end of next row, then 1 st at
each end of foll 4th rows 5(8,14,17,20,23)times
[61(69,81,89,95,103)sts], then in foll 6th row/s
13(11,7,5,3,1)time/s [87(91,95,99,101,105)sts].
Work until work measures 41 cm from start of Graph A.
Shape raglan Cast off 3 sts at beg of next 2 rows
[81(85,89,93,95,99)sts].
Dec 1 st at each end of next and alt rows
35(37,35,35,34,36)times in all [11(11,19,23,27,27)sts], then in
every row 1(1,5,7,9,9)time/s [9 sts]. Cast off.

FRONT BANDS

Button Band With right side facing Col 1 and 4.00mm
needles, pick up and K 115 sts from beg of front slope shaping
to picot row at lower edge of Left Front. Work 6 rows st st,
beg with a P row.
Change to Col 2, P1 row.
Change to 3.25mm needles.
Next row (picot row) K1, * yf, K2tog, rep from * to end. P1
row. Work 7 rows st st, beg with a K row and foll Graph B
(rows 1 to 7) for colour changes. Cast off loosely purlways
with Col 2.

Buttonhole Band With right side facing Col 1 and 4.00mm
needles, pick up and K115 sts from picot row at lower edge of
Right Front to beg of front slope shaping. Work 2 rows st st,
beg with a purl row.
Make buttonholes Next row P24, cast off 3 sts, (P18, cast off
3 sts) 4 times, P4.
Next row K4 turn, cast on 3 sts turn, (K18 turn, cast on 3 sts
turn)4 times, K24.
Work 2 rows st st, beg with a P row.
Change to Col 2, P1 row.
Change to 3.25mm Needles.
Next row (picot row) K1, * yf, K2tog, rep from * to end.
Purl 1 row.
Work rows 1 - 7 following Graph B, working buttonholes as
before on Rows 4 & 5.
Cast off loosely Purlways with Col 2.

MAKING UP

Press all pieces, very gently on WS using a warm iron over a
damp cloth. Using Backstitch, join raglan seams, noting that
tops of sleeves form part of neckline. Join side and sleeve
seams, leaving opening at side seams for pocket openings
between 9 and 25cm from picot edge.
Pocket Edgings With right side facing, using 3.25mm
Needles and Col 1, pick up and K 35 sts evenly along front
edge of pocket opening.
Next row Purl.
Next row (picot row) K1, * yf, K2tog, rep from * to end.
Work 7 rows st st, beg with a purl row. Cast off loosely
knitways. Fold pocket edgings on to wrong side at picot row
and slip stitch in position.
Left Front Pocket Lining Using 4.00mm Needles and Col 1,
cast on 36 sts. Work 40 rows st st. Dec 1 st at end of next and
alt rows 7 times in all [29 sts], then in every row 11 times
[18sts]. Cast off. Right Front Pocket Lining Using 4.00mm
Needles and Col 1, cast on 36 sts. Work 40 rows st st. Dec 1
st at beg of next and alt rows 7 times in all [29 sts], then in
every row 11 times [18 sts]. Cast off. With right sides tog and
using Backstitch, sew last 48 rows along straight side of pocket
linings to back edge of pocket openings. Slipstitch rem of
pocket linings to wrong side of fronts, sewing first 16 rows on
straight side of pocket linings to side seams.
Fold all hems to wrong side at Picot row and slip stitch into
position matching buttonholes and leaving front bands open at
neck edge. Oversew buttonholes. Sew on buttons.
Collar Using 3.25mm needles and Col 1, cast on
163(171,171,179,179,187)sts. Work 7 rows st st, change to
Col 2, purl 1 row.
Next Row (Picot row) K 1, *yf K2 tog, rep from * to end.
Next Row, P dec 1 st at end of row
162(170,170,178,178,186)sts.
Change to 4.00mm needles, using st st beg with a K row, foll
graph B for col changes. Work 8 rows.
Shape collar Keeping patt correct, cast off 2 sts at beg of next
18(14,14,10,10,6)rows [126(142,142,158,158,174)sts], then 3 sts
at beg of next 20(24,24,28,28,32)rows [66(70,70,74,74,78sts].
Next row Using Col 1, *K 2 tog, rep from * to end
[33(35,35,37,37,39)sts]. Work 1 row. Cast off.
Place wrong side of collar to right side of jacket and oversew
shaped edge of collar to neckline. Fold hem on collar onto
wrong side at picot row and slipstitch in position, grafting
collar hem to top edges of frontbands. Press seams and hems.

How to care for your pure wool knitwear

Knitting with Jo Sharp Pure Wool is 'Investment Knitting'.

Spun from premium grade long fibre fleece, the Jo Sharp garment you create this year will, with care, become a trusted favourite in the years to come. Jo Sharp yarn knits into a hard-wearing item of clothing that is beautifully warm and soft. It is not surprising that Jo's wool performs so well when you consider it has survived all the elements while still on the sheep's back. It is practical, long-lasting and natural. We can promise you that a Jo Sharp wool garment will stand up to harsh outdoor conditions whilst keeping its softness and good looks throughout years of wear.

Wool knitwear requires care and attention when it is washed, however it does not soil easily and requires maintenance less frequently than any other fibre.

Why Jo chose not to machine wash treat her yarn

Jo Sharp Hand Knitting Yarn has a natural crimp and elasticity which makes it satisfying to knit with. Its waxy outer coating of tiny overlapping scales, (rather like roof shingles) repel liquids and particles of dust or dirt. Wool contains millions of tiny pockets of air which act as natural thermal insulators. Unfortunately, machine wash treatment puts an artificial resin coating on wool fibres, effectively gluing them together and damaging natural thermal characteristics. This treatment also gives wool yarn an un-natural shiny appearance. For these reasons, Jo Sharp chose not to machine wash treat her yarn.

To further enhance Jo Sharp yarn

Inferior short fibres (which can cause pilling and itching) are removed during processing. This treatment improves the yarn's natural softness and wash and wear performance. With care, your quality Jo Sharp garment will improve with age and wear.

What causes wool knitwear to shrink?

Nature designed the wool fibre to be a protective coating for sheep in all weather. The unique outer layer or scale structure of the wool fibre resists soiling, but is also the reason why wool shrinks when not cared for properly. With severe agitation or tumble drying, the scales on the fibre lock together causing the garment to reduce in size and become thick and fluffy (felted). If you carefully follow the washing instructions on the inside of the Jo Sharp yarn label and opposite, you should not encounter any problems with shrinkage.

Hand Washing

For the best result, turn garment inside out and gently hand wash in lukewarm water, using a wool detergent. Rinse thoroughly in lukewarm water. Rinse again in cold water.

Drying

To remove excess moisture after washing, roll garment inside a large towel and gently squeeze or, alternatively, spin dry inside a pillow case. Never tumble dry. Place garment on a flat surface in the shade to dry, coaxing it back into shape whilst damp. Drying flat is recommended, but if using a clothes line, fold the garment over to prevent stretching. Don't peg it up like a shirt. On heavy garments, sleeves can be pegged up. Do not dry directly in front of an open or artificial fire.

Machine washing

If care is taken, a garment may be successfully machine washed. Turn the garment inside out and place inside a sealed pillow slip. Use a wool detergent and a gentle cycle with a medium spin and lukewarm water. Any severe agitation may shrink your garment. Dry as above.

Dry cleaning

Generally is not recommended as residual dry cleaning chemicals tend to harden wool fabric.

Combing

When our extra long fibre yarn is processed, most of the short fibres are removed. If, in the first few weeks of wear, a few remaining short fibres shed, these should be combed from your garment using a "de-piller" comb. De-pilling combs are generally inexpensive and are available from craft stores.

Yarn Specification

Jo Sharp 8ply DK Pure Wool Hand Knitting Yarn is made from extra fine and soft 100% Merino/Border Leicester fleece.
(DK is the USA and UK equivalent of Australian 8 ply)
One Ball of yarn is 50g (1 3/4 oz)
and approx 98 Mtrs (107 yards) in length.
Tension/Gauge: 22.5 sts and 30 rows, measured over 10cm using 4.00 mm (UK 8) (USA 6) needles.

PURE NEW WOOL

JO SHARP

Hand Knitting Collection Stockists

AUSTRALIA

Head Office & Mail Order Enquiries
JO SHARP HAND KNITTING YARN
PO Box 357 Albany
Western Australia 6330
Ph +61 08 9842 2250 Fax +61 08 9842 2260
e.mail - josharp@albanyis.com.au
http://www.cybermall.com.au/josharp/

Australian Retail Stores
Enquiries
Coats Spencer Crafts
Private Bag 15
Mulgrave North
Victoria Australia 3171
Ph 03 9561 2288
Fax 03 9561 2298
Toll Free 1800 641 277

New South Wales
Armidale Wool Shop, Armidale (02 6772 7083)
Champion Textiles, Newtown (02 9519 6677)
Corrimal Kids Cottage, Corrimal (02 9744 0164)
Craftsmith, Castle Hill (02 9680 2241)
Greta's Handcraft Centre, Lindfield (02 9416 2489)
Jannette Smith Fabrics, Goulburn (02 4832 2160)
Knowing Yarn, Annandale (02 9564 0946)
Knit It, Eastwood (02 9874 1358)
Lady Ann, Woy Woy (02 4342 2249)
Longreach Stuga, Marulan (02 4841 1657)
Pins and Needles, Merimbula (02 6495 3646)
The Calico Connection, Wentworth Falls (02 4757 1352)
The Wool Inn, Penrith (02 4732 2201)
The Wool Shack, Bathurst (02 6332 9223)
Australian Capital Territory
Shearing Shed, Kingston (02 6295 0061)
Stitch 'n' Time, Mawson (02 6286 4378)
Queensland
Miller & Coates, Ascot (07 3268 3955)
Tasmania
Knitters of Australia, Moonah (03 6229 6052)
Needle & Thread, Devonport (03 6424 6920)
The Needlewoman, Hobart (03 6234 3966)
The Spinning Wheel, Hobart (03 6234 1711)
Wool Place, Glenorchy (03 6272 3313)
Victoria
Audrey's Wool Shop, Altona (03 9938 9293)
Bayswater Wool Centre, Bayswater (03 9729 6915)
Healesville Art & Craft, Healesville (03 5962 2266)
Jeanette's Wool Shop, Carnegie (03 9569 9527)
Knight's Habby, Kyabram (03 5852 2862)
Knit & Purl Warehouse, Dandenong (03 9793 3530)

Marra Emporium, Reservoir (03 9469 4400)
Montrose Wool & Crafts, Montrose (03 9728 6437)
Monty's Wool Shop, Montmorency (03 9434 4746)
Mooroolbark Craft & Habby, Mooroolbark (03 9726 7291)
Mornington Wool Centre, Mornington (03 5975 4247)
Mylady's, Melbourne (03 9654 6509)
Pingvin, Maffra (03 5147 2135)
Purl Plain & Petit Point, Portland (03 5523 6044)
Rangeview Craft, Mitcham (03 9874 3037)
Simply Wool, Warrandyte (03 9844 1744)
Singer Sewing Centre, Colac (03 5231 3252)
Sunbury Wool Centre, Sunbury (03 9744 4520)
The Stitchery, Essendon (03 9379 9790)
Warrnambool Wool & Uniforms, War'bool (03 5562 9599)
Wool 'n' Things, East Keilor (03 9331 0910)
Wool Village, Mulgrave (03 9560 5869)
Wool Shed Crafts, Rosanna (03 9432 1820)
Western Australia
Anne's Machine Knitting Shop, Rockingham (08 9527 1606)
Crossway's Wool & Fabrics, Subiaco (08 9381 4286)
Hanover Bay Emporium, Albany (08 9842 1277)

CANADA
Wholesale Enquiries
Estelle Designs
Units 65/67 2220 Midland Ave.
Scarborough, Ontario M1P 3E6
Ph 416 298 9922 Fax 416 298 2429

Canadian Retail Stores
Alberta
Wool Revival, Edmonton (403 471 2749)
British Columbia
Boutique de Laine, Victoria (250 592 9616)
Greatest Knits, Victoria (250 386 5523)
Craft Cottage, Richmond (604 278 0313)
House of Wool, Prince George (604 562 2803)
Manitoba
Ram Wools, Winnipeg (204 942 2797)
The Sheep Boutique, Winnipeg (204 786 8887)
Ontario
Elizabeth's Wool Shop, Kitchener (519 744 1881)
Christina Tandberg Knits, London (519 672 4088)
London Yarns & Machines, London (519 474 0403)
Needles and Knits, Aurora (905 713 2066)
Muskoka Yarn Connection, Bracebridge (905 645 5819)
Passionknit Ltd, Toronto (416 322 0688)
Romni Wools, Toronto (416 703 0202)
The Celtic Fox, Toronto (416 487 8177)
The Hill Knittery, Richmond Hill (905 770 4341)
The Needle Emporium, Ancaster (905 648 1994)
The Yarn Tree, Streetsville (905 821 3170)
Village Yarns, Toronto (416 232 2361)
Imagiknit 2000, Orilla (705 689 8676)
Saskatchewan
The Wool Emporium, Saskatoon (306 374 7848)